HERO STORIES OF FRANCE

FERDINAND FOCH, MARSHAL OF FRANCE

HERO STORIES OF FRANCE

BY

EVA MARCH TAPPAN

WITH ILLUSTRATIONS

BOSTON AND NEW YORK
HOUGHTON MIFFLIN COMPANY
The Riverside Press Cambridge
1920

CONTENTS

ILLUSTRATIONS

HERO STORIES OF FRANCE

CHAPTER I

VERCINGETORIX, THE HERO PATRIOT

Two thousand years ago no one had ever heard the word "France," for the country that we call by that name was then known as "Gaul." It was larger than the France of to-day, for it extended to the Alps and the Rhine River.

On the sunny plains and in the pleasant valleys there were many little villages, mere groups of round huts made of poles bound together at the top, and probably plastered with clay to keep out the wind and cold. On the hills, however, there were often towns with streets of houses framed of stout timbers. There were workshops, too, and in these the Gauls made pottery, different sorts of weapons, and beautifully enameled jewelry.

The Gauls wore tunics of bright-colored plaids and, what seemed queerest to the Romans, they also wore trousers instead of the loosely draped robes or togas of Rome. The Romans actually spoke of the part of Gaul nearest to their own country as "the province that wears trousers." They were an enterprising people, these Gauls. They built roads from town to town, they laid bridges across the rivers, their heavily laden barges floated down the streams, and the largest vessels on the Mediterranean Sea belonged to Gallic owners. They had valuable mines, and they knew how to work them. They knew a good horse when they saw one, and whenever there was a well-bred steed for sale, there was always a Gaul ready to pay a high price for him.

Many different tribes lived in Gaul, and often there was warfare among them. Then the warriors put on their chain armor, their golden rings and armlets, and their helmets, each made in the shape of the head of some wild beast. They seized their pikes and swords and shields, mounted their prancing horses, and galloped off to battle, great plumes nodding over their helmets as they dashed onward.

In Italy, southeast of Gaul, lived the Romans, the most powerful nation of the age. They ruled nearly all the countries bordering on the Mediterranean Sea. Their capital city was Rome, and there, as in many more of their cities, they had handsome buildings, statues, gardens, robes of silk and the finest wool, jeweled cups, and all sorts of luxuries. Powerful as they were, the Romans felt uneasy when they thought of their Gallic neighbors. Three hundred years earlier, the Gauls had dashed down upon them and had burned their capital. The invaders had finally been driven away, but there was no knowing when they might come again. The Romans already controlled part of Gaul — including the province that wore trousers — and if they could only rule the whole country, they would sleep better nights.

In 58 B. C. the Romans were feeling especially uneasy, because the Germans, who lived on the shores of the Baltic and the North Seas, were breaking into Gaul, killing and destroying wherever they went. If they should succeed in overrunning this country, they would next attack Rome. Just at this time a tribe living in Switzerland decided to cross Gaul and settle near the Atlantic coast. The Gauls begged the Romans to prevent this. It was an excellent opportunity for the Romans, and Julius Cæsar was sent to Gaul with an army.

Cæsar soon obliged the Swiss to return to their old homes; and then he set out to make it clear to the Germans that they would not be allowed to remain in Gaul. He sent to the German chief Ariovistus and asked him to name a place for a parley. The independent young man sent back the message, "If I wanted anything of you, I should go where you were; and if you want anything of me, you must come where I am." "I am ready to be a good friend to you," returned Cæsar, "but you may be sure that I shall not overlook any injury to the people of Gaul." "If you want to fight," declared Ariovistus, "choose your own time and come on." Cæsar did "come on," and he drove the Germans back over the Rhine.

Now the Gauls were bright people, keen and wide-awake. They began to suspect that Cæsar meant not only to drive away the Germans, but to conquer Gaul, and they had no idea of giving up their freedom. Year after year the struggle between Cæsar and the Gauls went on. At length Gaul seemed to be completely subdued, and Cæsar ventured to return to Rome for a short time. This was just the moment for a revolt, and a young chief called Vercingetorix aroused the other chiefs to unite against the invaders. These chiefs chose him to be their leader. Then they stacked their standards and took a solemn oath to be true to their country and to one another.

But when Cæsar returned they soon found out that they could not withstand him in open battle. "We must starve him out," declared Vercingetorix to his people. "There are a few towns that we can defend, but every other town and even every village that contains any store of grain must be burned to the ground. This is not an easy thing for you to do, but would it be easier to give up your own lives and have your wives and children sold as slaves?" "No, no," the people shouted, and before the sun had set, twenty villages were already smouldering in their ruins. "Let them burn!" cried the Gauls; "we shall soon have better ones."

But the people of the town Avaricum begged that their city might be spared. "It is one of the finest towns in all Gaul," they pleaded, "and there is a marsh on three sides which will serve us well in defense." Vercingetorix yielded, though unwillingly, and Avaricum was not destroyed.

It was not long before the Romans appeared at the end of a causeway which led across the marsh nearly to Avaricum. They continued this causeway by adding a strong wooden terrace, 330 feet wide and 80 feet high; and on this they built stout sheds of heavy logs, their roofs covered with clay, and also built a high fence or screen. Both sheds and fence were on rollers and were pushed nearer and nearer to the town as the work progressed. They began also a high tower from which the slingers and archers could shoot.

The Gauls, too, had been building towers, and these stood, well filled with soldiers, all along the wall of the town. This wall was too strong for any battering ram to make a hole in it, and as it was built chiefly of stones, it could not be set on fire. Therefore the Romans clutched the great stones with stout hooks and pulled them down; that is, they tried to pull them down, but the Gauls had a discouraging fashion of letting down nooses to catch the hooks, and then pulling them up over the wall. They had another custom which was even more disagreeable, for they poured streams of boiling pitch down upon the heads of their enemies. Nevertheless, the Romans kept hard at work till the tower was nearly finished. Suddenly, a slender thread of smoke was seen, then there was a tongue of fire, and then the woodwork of the terrace burst into flames, for some of the Gauls had been burrowing under it and had set it afire.

Now the Gauls poured out of the gates. A fierce battle was waged, and Avaricum was taken. The Gauls, old men, women, and children, were cut down without mercy. Out of more than forty thousand, only eight hundred escaped. These managed to make their way to the camp of Vercingetorix, a few miles distant. "Keep your courage," the wise young leader pleaded. "No one can expect to have success always. If Gaul is only united, the whole world cannot overcome her." The men shouted and clashed their arms in applause, and Vercingetorix set out at once to persuade as many tribes as possible to unite with him against the Roman invaders.

The Gauls fought savagely for their freedom, but at length the time came when they had to withdraw to the hill town of Alesia. Vercingetorix had foreseen that this might be necessary, and therefore he had fortified the town and stored it with provisions, so that if the worst came to the worst, he could retreat to it for a last stand.

On the day after the Gallic leader took possession of Alesia, the watchman on the walls reported, "Cæsar and his troops are encamped before the town. They are digging trenches and heaping up great mounds of earth for the archers." The Romans worked by day, and by night, too, when the moon was up. They tapped rivers and filled some of the trenches with water. They hid sharp-pointed logs and barbed spikes in low brushwood, and they made a ring of camps nearly around the town. Soon the brave defenders would be entirely shut in.

Vercingetorix now called his cavalry apart. "The Roman works will soon be completed," he said, "and if we are ever to get help, now is our chance. Do you steal out of the city to-night, and go, every one of you, to his home town. Tell your people that they must stand by us, and when you come back, bring with you every man that can wield a sword. I will do my best to make the food last a month longer. Go." That night the Gauls slipped out silently from the town and stole up the valleys into the darkness, each going the shortest way to his home town.

The days passed, and little food remained. Vercingetorix watched anxiously for the return of the cavalry. But they had gone on a difficult errand. Some of the tribes were jealous; some were defending themselves from the Germans in their own home towns; some had already yielded to Rome; one tribe declared that they intended to attack Cæsar by themselves, and had no idea of putting themselves under any one's command. There was much delay, but at length Vercingetorix saw a cloud of dust, and as the sun fell on it, the glitter of pikes. It was the cavalry with many thousands of helpers. Now was the time for a sortie. Vercingetorix had thought of everything. He had made movable huts to shelter his men as they moved forward. He had provided fascines to fill up the trenches. A fierce battle was fought, but the Gauls were at last driven back to Alesia.

Cæsar, then, was besieging Alesia, and beyond his ring of camps was a ring of Gauls who were besieging him. The fresh troops in the ring of Gauls stole silently out of their camp at midnight and drew closer to the Roman works. A sudden blare from their trumpets aroused their friends in the town. Fascines were tossed into the moats, stones flew from the slings, scaling ladders were thrown up, grappling hooks to pull down the ramparts were set to work. But the pointed logs and the spikes and the heavy pikes hurled down upon them by the Romans were more than they could meet, and again the Gauls had to withdraw.

But they did not give up. Once more they dashed upon the Roman forces from the rear, and Vercingetorix, coming down from the town rushed upon them from the front. The Gauls were more in number, but the Romans were more perfectly trained as soldiers. It began to grow dark, and the Gallic newcomers fled into the night. "Back to the town!" commanded Vercingetorix, for the fight was lost, his last struggle for the freedom of Gaul had been made. In the morning he called his chiefs together. "I have fought for my country," he said, "not for myself, but for all of you. We have lost, but it may be that my death will appease these angry Romans. Kill me if you think best, or give me up alive to Cæsar as a prisoner. Perhaps he will then spare you."

The other chiefs were men of less noble strain. They talked the matter over. "Vercingetorix will be slain in any case," they said. "To die with him would be of no good to us or to him. We may as well let his death save our own lives." So they sent messengers to Cæsar. "We yield," they said, "and we are ready to surrender to you Vercingetorix, the man who has been our leader in the revolt."

"Give up your arms," commanded Cæsar, "and let the under-chiefs come forth." Then the under-chiefs came out to Cæsar and bowed humbly before him as he sat on a tribunal or raised seat built on a fragment of the wall in front of his camp, and every chief said, "I promise to be faithful to you and to serve you." Then a trampling of hoofs was heard, and a handsome horse, splendidly caparisoned, galloped through the gateway of the city. On his back was Vercingetorix. Three times he rode around the tribunal; then he sprang lightly to the ground, took off his armor and laid it together with his sword on the ground before Cæsar, bowing himself at the feet of his conqueror. There he knelt, silently begging mercy for his people. Cæsar gazed at him for some moments, then ordered the guards to lead him away.

For six long years the noble Gallic patriot was kept in a dungeon at Rome. Then came the time of Cæsar's triumphal procession in honor of his victories. The great general rode in a superb chariot drawn by white horses. He wore a robe heavily embroidered with palm leaves, and on his head was a crown of laurel. An ivory scepter was in his hand. The senators of Rome formed his escort and conducted him through the city gates, through the streets, and up to the capitol. Before him were many wagons bearing the spoils of his warfare — gold, silver, precious stones, jewelry and other products, and handiwork of the conquered countries. Then came great models of the cities that had been captured, then long lines of captives, who had now become slaves of the Romans. Behind them walked the leaders whom Cæsar had subdued; and last of them all was the noble Vercingetorix, the man who loved his country better than himself, and who had given himself gladly in the struggle to win her freedom. Even the years in a Roman dungeon had not broken his spirit, and, loaded with chains as he was, he held himself proudly erect. Between him and his conqueror marched the legions of Roman soldiers, singing songs of victory. They were praised and rewarded; but the Gallic patriot was led back to his prison and put to death.

CHAPTER II

SAINT DENIS THE MISSIONARY

CAESAR was a pitiless enemy, but after the Gauls had once yielded, he treated them justly and kindly. Many of those nearest to Rome learned to talk Latin as if they had been born Romans, and to live quite in Roman fashion. They built handsome houses, temples, theaters, baths, and aqueducts. They learned how to drain the swamps and how to cultivate the soil so it would do its best. The Romans were always famous road-builders, and they taught the Gauls how to build the matchless stone roads that have lasted for centuries. Gallic schools were opened and libraries formed. The Gauls continued their old manufactures, and made also glass, silk, tapestry, and many other things; indeed, in some of their work they improved upon Roman methods. Everything went on prosperously.

But as the years passed, the Romans became idle and fond of luxury. If there was war, they were no longer eager to protect their country themselves, they preferred to pay others to fight for them. A great deal of money was called for, and taxes became very severe. The laws also became severe, until at length there was a law for almost every act and a heavy penalty for every violation. The Gauls had gained in order and civilization, but they had lost their freedom. Vercingetorix would have hardly recognized his country.

But something new and wonderful had come to pass. In a far-away little province of the Empire Jesus Christ was born, and his teachings made their way to Rome. Before this, both Gauls and Romans had worshiped many gods. They had gods of harvest, of springtime, of the sun, the moon, the rain, and the thunder. Missionaries and teachers now made their way into Gaul, and the wretched people learned that there was a God who cared for them and was sorry when they were unhappy.

Soon, however, the people who were rejoicing in this new faith found themselves in trouble with Rome. The Romans were perfectly willing that the Gauls should have as many gods as they chose, provided that they would now and then burn a few grains of incense before the images of some of the Roman gods or say a prayer before the statue of some emperor. To refuse to do this was looked upon as almost treason to the State; but, of course, no Christian could yield to any such command; therefore the Christians were terribly persecuted. Some were tortured and then slain; some were given to wild beasts to be devoured.

Nevertheless, the teaching of the Gospel spread, and missionaries continued to go to Gaul to teach and help the unhappy people. One of the most famous of these missionaries was Saint Denis. According to the old tradition, he set out from Rome with six companions. Perhaps he went over one of the Roman roads to Lyons, which was then the capital of Gaul; then partly by road and partly by rivers he pressed on, stopping every little while to talk to the natives about Jesus. "You pray to the sun and the moon," he would say, "but they do not hear your prayer. Let me tell you about the one true God, who listens when you pray and cares for you."

After a while Saint Denis came to a little town on the Seine River called Lutetia, or "the muddy place." This was the name it bore in Cæsar's time, three hundred years earlier; and, although it now had some excellent buildings and its people had been growing rich through the river traffic, it was still called by the same name.

The tribe living in this part of Gaul were called the Parisii. They listened eagerly to the preaching of Saint Denis and his companions. Many hundreds came to believe that what the missionaries said was true. "We will no longer worship the sun and the moon and the thunder," they declared. "We will make our prayers to the God of the preacher, for we believe that this is the one true God." They built a Christian church and rejoiced in their new faith.

Before long, however, the Roman emperor heard what was being done in the land of the Parisii, and he sent an officer to seize the missionaries and put them to death. The officer journeyed to Lutetia and called the preachers before him on the charge of teaching treason to the State. They were sentenced to be beheaded and were taken to Montjoie Hill, where the sentence was carried out. Their bodies were thrown into the river Seine, but a Christian woman recovered them and saw to it that they were buried with honor. A chapel was built over Saint Denis's tomb, and for more than a thousand years the French people used to shout "Montjoie Saint Denis!" whenever they were going into battle.

Some of the pictures of Saint Denis are just a bit startling, for they represent an angel holding a crown over the martyr, although the good saint has no head on which to put it. He is doing his best, however, to supply the deficiency, for he is quietly picking up his head from the ground. People forgot that the object of such a picture was to teach, so that when any one looked at it, he would recall the manner in which the saint met his death; and the legend arose that after Saint Denis's head was cut off, he picked it up and carried it in his arms two miles to his place of burial.

CHAPTER III

THE COMING OF ATTILA THE HUN

IN 312 the man who was then Roman emperor became a Christian, and of course this put an end to the persecutions of the Christians in Gaul. The Gauls had other troubles to meet, however, for the Germans were making raids across the Rhine into the Gallic lands. Lutetia had now become Paris, and here the Roman governor made his home, so that he could keep watch of the invaders.

Rome grew weaker and weaker, and at length the Romans almost gave up fighting with the Germans and made alliances with some of them instead, calling them friends and guests and actually allowing them — perhaps even inviting them — to come over the Rhine and make their homes in Gaul. They expected the newcomers, to whom they had shown such favor, to prevent the rest of the Germans from entering the land, but they were disappointed. The lands of Gaul were more fertile than those farther north, the climate was warmer, and the sky clearer, and the Germans continued to come. One group of tribes in particular, the Franks, or "Free Men," were especially bold and daring, and it was soon plain that they had come to stay and that all Rome could not hinder them.

Before long the time came when even the Gauls were glad of the presence of these fierce warriors. On winter evenings, in the dimly lighted homes of Gaul, fearsome tales began to be told of a terrible race known as Huns. "They are coming from Scythia," whispered the story-tellers fearfully. "They are coming on horseback, and they are bringing in great carts their women and all their treasures. They have tiny black eyes, flat faces, and broad noses. Their ears flare out from their heads, their skins are painted and tattooed. They have no beards, but their hair is rough and shaggy. Their bodies are short and square, and when they walk, they look like bears trying to stand on two legs. People say that their mothers were witches, their fathers demons, and that they know how to work all kinds of evil spells upon their enemies." "But cannot the emperor buy them off?" some one would ask; and the answer was, "The emperor has already given them land and promised to pay them tribute; but no one believes that they will stay where he put them."

They did not stay, but pressed on into Gaul; and now the Gauls were glad of the help of Romans, Franks, and any one else who could wield a sword. Led by their chief Attila, the Huns swept on, killing and destroying wherever they went. "Grass never grows again where the hoofs of Attila's steed have trod," was the old saying.

Attila claimed that his sword had come to him as a gift from the god of war. It seemed, according to the legend, that one of the Hun shepherds noticed that blood was dropping from the foot of a young heifer.

He traced her footsteps back to a place where he saw a sharp point sticking up out of the ground, and found that it was the point of an ancient sword. He carried the sword to Attila. "This is the sword of the god of war," declared the wily leader. "The gods have sent it to me, and wherever I wield it, there we shall win a victory."

It began to seem as if Attila had made a true prophecy, for the chief with his Huns ran through country after country, successful almost everywhere. "The Scourge of God," he was afterward called. He and his savage followers were galloping straight for Paris, and the people of that city were just beginning a frantic flight for somewhere, they knew not where, in the hope of saving their lives, when suddenly the doors of the church were flung open, and a young maiden stood before them. The people fell on their knees before her, for this was Genevieve, a shepherd girl whose holiness they all knew. "I have called the holy matrons and the consecrated virgins to come together in the church," she said, "and I have bidden them to pray earnestly and trustfully to God that he will save our city. He has listened to our prayers. Go back to your houses, for Paris will be saved."

This is the legend that has come down through the years. Whether it is true or not, it is a fact that Attila suddenly changed his course; Paris was spared, and he drove on to Orleans.

Orleans had new and strong fortifications, and her people had no thought of yielding. But after a while food began to be scanty, the walls showed cracks made by Attila's battering rams, and the Huns were drawing closer and closer around the city. The citizens of Orleans knew that Romans, Gauls, Franks, and others were trying to come together to meet the Huns, but there was long delay in their coming, and perhaps they would not come at all.

"Be brave and do not let your courage fail," said the good Bishop of Orleans to his people. "Here is the messenger whom I sent to the lookout on the rampart. Have you good news for us?" he asked, turning to the young man.

"Alas, no!" he replied. "I could see nothing but the great plain stretching out to the horizon."

"Go once more," bade the bishop, and the young man went again.

"Are they coming?" asked the bishop when he returned.

"Alas, no!" replied the young man for the second time. "There is nothing to be seen but the great plain."

"Go yet a third time, my son," said the bishop. "God's aid sometimes seems slow, but it is sure."

So the young man went a third time, and when he came back his face was so bright that the people knew he had brought good news.

"The great plain stretches out as before," he said, "but far away on the horizon there is a tiny cloud."

"The armies are coming! It is the aid of the living God!" cried the bishop; and the multitude said after him in hushed and reverent tones, "it is the aid of the living God."

So the people of Orleans fought more bravely than ever, and soon Attila too saw the cloud, then the gleam of the shining pikes, then the banners, and last, the thousands of strong fighters coming to the rescue of the city.

Evidently a battle was at hand that would need all his forces, and Attila withdrew at once to the plain of the Marne River where Châlons now stands, brought all his troops together, and fortified his camp, arranging a breastwork of wagons around it. Then he spoke to his followers:

"Do you see our enemies coming upon us?" he asked, pointing to the advancing lines. "From one end of Europe to the other, armies have fled before us, and these people too will flee. Glorious deeds await you and mighty will be your rewards. Be brave. Be fearless, and show our enemies the valor of the Huns!" "On! On! Lead us on!" cried the Huns, shouting their battle-cries and rushing forward upon the Gallic lines.

Terrible fighting went on all that day, and only ceased when the combatants could no longer see one another's faces. Attila withdrew to the shelter of the camp with its barricade of wagons and its intrenchments and made ready for another battle on the morrow. "No man shall ever boast of having captured Attila, the Scourge of God!" he declared, and he built up a great mound of the wooden saddles of his cavalry. On this he poured out his most valuable treasures, and around it he stationed his wives. "If our enemies should be on the point of taking the camp," he said, "I shall set fire to this pile and perish with my treasures. Neither I nor these shall ever fall into the hands of our foes."

When the morning came, the battle went on again, so furiously that, even after the fighting had ceased, people could hardly believe that it had really come to a close, and the legend quickly arose that high up in the clouds above the field of slaughter the spirits of the slain continued for three days the dreadful struggle. The Gauls and their aids were the victors, but they made no attempt to destroy the invaders. Attila and his followers were allowed to withdraw toward Germany.

One year later the Huns invaded Italy and overcame city after city. The terrible Hun, savage as he was, had a sense of humor. In one of the Italian cities Attila came upon a picture representing the Roman emperors sitting on their thrones, while the princes of Scythia bowed at their feet. Attila sent for a painter. "Change that," he commanded. "Put *me* on the throne and paint the emperors pouring out their gold at *my* feet."

Attila was planning more invasions when he suddenly died. His followers raised a great silken pavilion and within it they laid the body of their leader. Around this marched the lines of the Huns, chanting a funeral hymn of praise and sorrow. "He was glorious in his life," they sang, "and in his death he was invincible. To his people he was a father, to his enemies a scourge, and to the whole world a dread and terror." They cut off locks of their hair and they made jagged cuts into their faces that the blood might flow freely; for they said, "The tears wept for such a man should not be of water but of blood." They then laid him into a coffin of iron, next into one of silver, and last into one of gold. Lest these should be stolen and his body be treated with disrespect, they buried him at dead of night, putting into his grave a quantity of weapons and treasures. The grave was filled up, and the prisoners who had dug it were put to death, that no one should know where the mighty Scythian leader had been laid. Then, according to their custom, they held a great feast with song and jest and merriment.

This battle of Châlons, the true "first battle of the Marne," is famous for two reasons. The first is because it was so fierce and so many men were engaged in it. The second is because on the plains of Châlons it was settled that the Huns, heathen and barbarians, should not rule in Europe.

CHAPTER IV

CLOVIS, THE FIRST KING OF FRANCE

WHILE there was danger from the Huns, the different tribes stood together, but when that danger was past, each people began to consider how they could make themselves more powerful than the others.

Of all the Franks that had come into Gaul, the Salii, or Salian Franks, were the strongest, although as yet they held only a little land on the left bank of the Rhine. Their chief, Meroveus, had fought at Châlons. In 481, thirty years after this battle, Meroveus and his son were both dead, and the only one left to represent his family was a boy of fifteen named Clovis. He was a strong, energetic boy, and young as he was, he had already shown on the battle-field that he could strike a hard blow and a skillful one. The Frankish warriors voted that he should be their chief. "Clovis! Clovis!" they shouted, and they carried him through their villages raised high up on their shields, so that every one might know whom they had chosen.

Clovis was an ambitious young man, and he promptly set about increasing his territory. When he was only twenty, he defeated the Romans at Soissons, about sixty miles from Paris. Other towns soon fell into his hands, and so he became master of a wide area in what is now northern France.

There were always many treasures in the churches, and among those taken from the church in Rheims there was an especially beautiful golden vase. Now the young chief had taken a liking to the Bishop of Rheims, and the bishop was very willing to have the good-will of the valiant young heathen. He would have it in his power to show many a favor to the Church, and some day he might even become a Christian.

So it was that, when Clovis and his followers were about to divide the booty, a messenger from the bishop appeared. He earnestly besought Clovis to return what had been taken from the church at Rheims, "or, if that is impossible," said the messenger, "to return at least the golden vase." Now, among the Franks, all booty was divided by lot, and the chief received no more than any one of his followers. Clovis spoke to his men. "Will you grant me the favor," said he, "of giving me the vase of Soissons besides what comes to me by lot?" Either the followers of Clovis were willing to please their leader or else they did not care to offend so powerful a man, for all but one agreed. That one, a surly fellow, growled out, "You will have what the lot gives you and nothing more." He raised his battle-axe and struck the vase a heavy blow. Clovis gave the man one look, then, without a word, he picked up the broken vase and handed it to the messenger.

Before long, the time came for his revenge. He was inspecting the arms and armor of his men, and when he came to the one who had broken the vase, he said, "There is no other man who has brought to me arms so poorly cared for as yours. You are not fit to be among my followers." He snatched the battle-axe from the man's hand and flung it down upon the ground. The warrior stooped to pick it up — perhaps that he might strike the first blow — but, however that may be, Clovis was before him. He gave his own axe a mighty swing and brought it down with deadly force upon the man's skull, crying, "This is what you did to the vase at Soissons."

Clovis had no wife, but he had heard stories which interested him in a young princess, Clotilde, niece of the King of Burgundy. It was said that this king had slain the rest of her family save one sister, who had entered a convent. Clotilde was living quietly at Geneva, giving all her time to deeds of charity. Of course Clovis knew that her uncle would not allow any suitor to have a glimpse of her, lest she should marry and thus gain power to avenge her family; so he gave his ring to a man whom he could trust and said: "Do you dress yourself in rags like a beggar and put a beggar's wallet upon your back. Go to Clotilde and say that you are on a pilgrimage and ask for her charity. If the stories told of her are true, she will not refuse to see a pilgrim, and you can give her my message and the ring."

The pretended beggar went to Geneva, and the gentle princess gave him food and washed his feet with her own royal hands. As she was bending over him, he leaned toward her and whispered, "Lady, Clovis, King of the Franks, would gladly offer you marriage. In proof of my words he sends you his ring."

Clotilde was glad. She rewarded the beggar and gave him a ring of her own to carry to the king. "If Clovis would wed me," she said, "let him send messengers without an instant's delay to demand me of my uncle and take me away with them. My uncle's chief counselor is now in Constantinople, and if he should return, he would advise against my marriage, especially with so powerful a man as the King of the Franks, lest I avenge the death of my family."

The moment that Clovis heard this, he sent an embassy to ask for Clotilde. The wicked uncle did not dare to refuse, so the ceremonies of espousal were gone through with, and the princess was put into a covered chariot drawn by four white oxen, and they set out with much dignity and splendor for the home of Clovis.

They had gone only a little way before a good friend of Clotilde's sent her a message. She called her escort together and said: "I have certain knowledge that the chief counselor has returned, and that my uncle has already sent out a troop of warriors in pursuit of me. If you would obey your king's command and carry me safely to him, do you get me as fast a horse as can be found." So it was that the bride of King Clovis entered Soissons, not in the glory of a chariot drawn by four white oxen, but on the back of a horse galloping at full speed.

This is the story that has come down to us of the marriage of Clovis and Clotilde. Very likely some of the praises of the princess that first interested Clovis in her came from the wise Bishop of Rheims, who would of course be delighted to have the powerful King of the Franks become the husband of a Christian maiden.

Clotilde did her best to persuade Clovis to become a Christian. "You worship gods of wood or stone or metal," she said. "They are nothing, and they can do nothing for you." "They made all things in the world," insisted Clovis sturdily. By and by a little son was born to them, and now Clotilde pleaded again with her husband. He did not yield, but he did promise that the little prince might be baptized. This was done, and Clotilde was happy. But in a few days the baby died. "That is what this baptizing has brought about," said Clovis. "If he had been dedicated to my gods, he would be alive. The gods are angry with me, and they have taken my child."

Clotilde was broken-hearted, but she would not give up her God, and when a second little son was born, she insisted that he, too, should be baptized. In a few days this child also fell sick. "His brother was baptized in the name of this Christ of yours," declared the king bitterly, "and he died. This child has been baptized, and he, too, will die." The child did not die, however, but grew well and strong, and Clovis began to think that after all it might be that baptism did not harm him.

A little while after this, Clovis was setting out for what he knew would be a terrible battle. He hoped for the help of his gods, but he was beginning to question a little whether they were really as powerful as he had supposed. As he was starting, Clotilde put her arms around his neck and said: "Your gods cannot help you to win this battle, but my God can. Will you promise me that if you are successful, you will thank my God and become a Christian?"

Clovis promised and said farewell. The battle was going against him, and even his most trusted fighters lost heart. The king remembered his promise and he cried out: "Jesus Christ, whom my queen Clotilde calls the Son of God, my old gods have failed me, and I come to Thee. Only give me victory over these enemies of mine, and I will believe in Thee and be baptized in Thy name."

The victory was won. Clovis kept his word, and when Christmas Day came, he went to Rheims to be baptized. The whole city rejoiced. All along the road leading from the palace to the cathedral, the houses were hung with tapestry and banners and draperies of brilliant colors. First in the procession came the clergy, bearing the book of the Four Gospels, the cross, and the standards, and chanting as they walked. Then came the Bishop of Rheims, leading the king by the hand. Close behind them walked the queen, and then came the long line of citizens and men at arms. When the moment for the baptism had come, a fair white dove fluttered in through the open window, hovered over the altar a moment, and then flew away. From this the legend arose that a dove had brought a vial of holy oil with which to anoint the king.

The two sisters of Clovis and three thousand of his men at arms were also baptized. He soon received from the Pope the title of "Most Christian King and Eldest Son of the Church," and this title has been handed down to every sovereign of France.

Clovis was not exactly what would in these days be called a "Most Christian King," for he aimed chiefly at conquering more land and murdering every one who might stand in the way of his power. The kingdom now included the greater part of Gaul. It began to be called Francia, or the country of the Franks. Its capital was Paris.

Thus it was that Clovis founded the French monarchy, and also Christian France, even though he was not the ideal Christian of to-day.

CHAPTER V

CHARLES THE HAMMER

When Clovis died, his kingdom was divided among his four sons, and every one of them was as determined to gain power as his father had been. They quarreled and they fought, and before long one of them was killed in battle. His three little boys went to live with their grandmother, Clotilde, and she did her best to hold their father's part of the kingdom for them.

The two uncles pretended to be fond of the boys and spread the report that they were going to put them upon their father's throne. Clotilde was delighted, and when the children were sent for, she made a great feast, dressed the boys in royal robes, and sent them to their uncles. But in a little while a stern man with a hard, cruel face appeared before Clotilde. "Lady Queen," he said, "I am sent here by your two sons. Your grandsons are in their hands, and I am to ask which of these you will choose for them." He held up in one hand a naked sword, and in the other a pair of shears.

Clotilde knew well what this meant. The sword was a sign of death; the shears of disgrace. Meroveus, who fought at the battle of Châlons, had long yellow hair, and this had come to be looked upon as a sure mark of royalty. To cut it off was the same as saying, "This man is not worthy of the crown. He must go away and hide himself in a monastery."

Poor Clotilde was frantic with grief. She exclaimed, "Better die than be shorn!" She could not think that her sons would be so wicked; but the messenger hurried away to them, and on the instant two of the little boys were slain. An attendant rescued the third child, and carried him away to safety in a convent. When he grew up, he became a monk of his own choice.

So the reigns of the Merovingian kings went on, marked by robbery, cruelty, and murder. The best among them was Dagobert, who came to the throne in 628. He was good-natured and really seemed to care for the love of his people; and this was something so new that his subjects called him "good King Dagobert." He used to go about through his kingdom, stopping at the principal places, and holding a sort of court of justice. It was a rough-and-ready variety of justice, but people soon found that he meant to be as fair to a poor man as to a rich man, and this was a great surprise and delight to them.

Dagobert may not have been an especially wise man, but he was wise enough to surround himself with good counselors and to listen to their words. He was interested in beautiful things, and the doughty soldier really enjoyed the exquisite work of Eloi, his treasurer, who had been a famous goldsmith before he became a monk. He made among other things a crown and scepter and a wonderful golden chair or throne richly adorned with jewels. He also did much work for the church which Dagobert built in honor of Saint Denis. Many years earlier, as has been said before, a little church or chapel had been built over the saint's grave; but it had become so dilapidated that one day a deer, trying to escape from the king, had no trouble in springing into the ruin. "It has gone to the good Saint Denis for refuge," said the king, "and it shall not be harmed." The frightened deer was allowed to go free, and in memory of this day the king built a church and abbey on the spot. Here was kept the sacred oriflamme, or "golden flame." This was a small banner of red silk, cut into two or three points. Whenever a French king was about to set out for war, he always went first to Saint Denis for this banner, and after the abbot had blessed it and prayed that it might never see defeat, it was delivered to him. In battle it was borne before him, and when there was any lull in the warfare, it stood before his tent. King Dagobert was buried in his beautiful church, and for more than a thousand years it was used as a tomb for all French kings.

Dagobert was the last king of the line of Meroveus who was good for anything. Twelve of his race followed him, but their names are not worth remembering. They had no ambition to get more land or even to rule what they had. They were stupid and lazy and roamed about in their ox-carts from one country house to another, eating and drinking heavily. The only thing about them that was royal was their long hair, and when one long-haired king over-ate himself and died, another took his place, and nobody knew the difference. People called them the "Do-Nothing" kings, and no one has ever found a better name for them.

Useless as these kings really were, there were certain things that they had to do, or pretend to do. One of these duties was to receive ambassadors from other lands. When one came to pay his respects to the king, the Do-Nothing would sit on the throne, try his best to look wise, and then repeat whatever words he was told to say.

The one whose orders he obeyed was called the "mayor of the palace." He was the "power behind the throne," and had to be a keen, bright man in order to fill the place. As the kings grew weaker, this officer grew stronger; and at length he even told the king how much pocket money he might be permitted to spend. If a king seemed at all inclined to be troublesome and disobedient, the mayor saw to it that he was poisoned or assassinated, or the people would be informed that the king was tired of his many cares and had decided to become a monk.

The Frankish kingdom had become so large that it extended far beyond the Rhine and included the whole of the present France except Brittany. It was not all at peace, and when one Charles came into power as mayor of the palace, he had some disorders to quell. It was not long, however, before matters in the kingdom were in good shape, for Charles was a strong, powerful ruler.

It was fortunate for France that such a man was in control, for greater trouble was coming from the

East than had ever threatened the country before, save in the days of the Huns. About two hundred years earlier, an Arabian named Mohammed had declared that God had sent him as a prophet. He produced a book called the Koran, which, he said, God had inspired him to write. At first slowly, then rapidly, his religion spread, until all Arabia had accepted it. Mohammed now declared that God had given him permission to make converts by the use of the sword. He sent missionaries to Persia, and when the people of that country would have nothing to do with him, he opened war upon them. He planned an attack upon Syria and the Roman Empire; but died before this could be undertaken.

Two hundred years after Mohammed died, his followers set out to conquer the world. It began to seem as if they would succeed; for they subdued Egypt and northern Africa, and then crossed over into Spain and Provence. Wherever they went, churches were robbed or torn down and Bibles were destroyed. They were savage fighters, and they swept all before them. Sometimes they accepted tribute, but generally they would say to their prisoners: "The choice is yours, the Koran or the sword. Believe in Mohammed or be slain."

These were the people who were already in Spain and southern France and had made their plans to sweep through the whole of France, Germany, and Italy. They came over the Pyrenees, crossed the Garonne River, and captured Bordeaux. The Mohammedans had heard of the wealth of Bordeaux, but they found it far greater than they had supposed. Their own stories of the capture declare that even the soldiers of lowest rank had plenty of precious stones, topazes, emeralds, and others; and that the whole army was so loaded down with gold and other booty that the marching became slow and stumbling.

To the people of Aquitania, however, the march of the Mohammedans seemed far too rapid. They had already covered the country between the Garonne and the Loire and had pushed into Burgundy. "Will you help me?" said Eudes, Duke of Aquitania, to Charles. "It is for your own good as well as mine. Let but these heathen crush Aquitania, and you and your Franks will next know their fury."

Charles was more than willing, and with his ready Franks he went at full speed to the Loire River. The city of Tours on the Loire was one of the richest in the whole land, and he was sure that the Mohammedans would try to capture it. He was right. "We will go to Tours," said the Mohammedan leaders, "and we shall find in the abbey there such treasures as no army ever took before."

If there had been such a thing as wireless telegraphy in those days, the Mohammedans would have known that trouble was before them; but they went on triumphantly to the very walls of Tours before they suspected that an enormous number of Franks were coming down upon them. Evidently this was no time to be dreaming about the treasures of Tours. Indeed, it would have been far better if they had tossed aside what loot they had already taken.

Probably neither side realized that this battle would decide whether Europe should be Christian or Mohammedan, but both did realize that it would be a tremendous struggle. Neither Charles nor the Mohammedan commander was eager to begin the fight. Time was not so valuable in those days, and for one whole week they waited and watched, each army in its own camp. At last, the Mohammedans made a general attack. The Franks "stood there," says one old writer, "like solid walls or icebergs." Another says that their hands were made of iron. They were tall and powerfully built, and their armor was stout and well made. Six days they fought in something like battle array. Then some of the Franks made a dash into the camp of the enemy. The Mohammedans rushed back from the general conflict to defend their camp. Everything became a wild turmoil, a fight between man and man; and here the height and strength of the Franks counted immensely. At night both armies always withdrew to their camps; but one morning no Mohammedans came out to renew the battle. Carefully the Franks went to reconnoiter. "It is a trick," said some of them, "and the heathen have hidden themselves in order to dash out upon us." But it was no trick; the Mohammedans had retreated in the night, and Europe was saved.

In this battle Charles had swung his heavy iron hammer or mace in such tremendous blows that after this he was known as Charles Martel, or "Charles the Hammer."

CHAPTER VI

PEPIN AND THE DO-NOTHING KINGS

CHARLES MARTEL did one good deed in overcoming the Mohammedans. He did another in bringing up his two sons so well that when the kingdom was left in their hands, they did not fight over it in a struggle for each to get the whole for himself, but worked together to do their best for the country. Before many years had passed, however, one of the sons became tired of ruling and entered a convent, leaving the possessions of both under the rule of his brother Pepin.

Pepin was a strong man, but of less than medium height, and people called him Pepin the Short. There was enough of him to make a king, but for some years he seemed to feel, like the rest of the Franks, that a people must have a Merovingian king, even if he did nothing but eat and drink and sit on a throne. Pepin discovered somewhere one of the royal family who seems to have been overlooked in spite of his long hair, and made a figurehead of him. Charles Martel had not been so careful of the prejudices of the Franks. *His* Merovingian had died or entered a convent, and Charles had never troubled himself to search for another, but had gone on ruling without one.

Pepin had a good deal of common sense, and after he had ruled for a few years with the Merovingian sitting on the throne and saying whatever he was told to say, he sent a messenger to the Pope to ask, "Who has the better right to be called king, the man who has the title or the man who rules?" "It is better that the man who rules should have the royal title," the Pope replied.

This settled the question as far as the monks and the clergy were concerned, but the masses of the people were still to be reckoned with. Pepin knew well that they would not be won by any reasoning, but by some showy feat of strength and fearlessness. It was a common and most cruel amusement to have fights between wild beasts or between beasts and men in great arenas, and one day when thousands were watching a lion attack a bull, Pepin waited until both were in a mad fury and the lion was getting the better of it; then, while people were watching in breathless silence, he rose and cried, "Which one among you dares to go and save that bull?" No one cared to try. Pepin waited a moment, then he himself leaped down into the arena, drew his sword, and, if we may trust the old story, cut off the lion's head at one blow. "Am I not worthy to be your king?" he demanded; and the people shouted: "Pepin! Pepin! He is worthy! King Pepin!" In the face of such a feat as this, the people had forgotten their old feeling that, no matter who ruled, a descendant of Meroveus must sit on the throne. The Frankish warriors raised Pepin on a shield, and the archbishop anointed him with the holy oil and placed the crown upon his head. The Franks were used to obeying Pepin's commands and following him in battle, and all went on as usual, no one caring in the least when the last of the long-haired Merovingians was taken away to a convent to spend the rest of his days.

The Pope had stood by Pepin, and now was the time to return the favor. The Lombards, a German people, had fought their way into northern Italy, had made settlements there, and were threatening to attack Rome. Stephen, who was now Pope, was too wise a man to be satisfied with sending a letter to Pepin. He was particularly anxious to win, not only the help, but the lasting friendship, of the king, and he crossed the Alps and journeyed to Paris. Pepin wished to do him all honor, for he, too, had a favor to ask; and he sent his son Charles, a manly young prince of twelve years, to represent him and give the Pope a cordial and brilliant reception.

Pope Stephen spent the winter at Saint Denis, winning friends wherever he went. Pepin promised to make an expedition against the Lombards, and the Pope promised to crown him a second time, for Pepin felt that his hold upon the throne would be stronger if the Pope himself had laid the crown upon his head. This the Pope did, in the cathedral at Rheims. He did it with generous thoroughness, for he anointed not only Pepin, but his two sons, Charles and his younger brother. He also gave Pepin the title of "Patrician of Rome."

Pepin now kept his part of the bargain, for he and his warriors went straight to Italy. "I demand that you evacuate the towns that you have seized," he declared, "and agree to leave Rome untouched." This the Lombards had no idea of doing, and now Pepin and his Franks came down upon them, overpowered them, and shut them up in Pavia. They were soon ready to promise anything and everything, and Pepin went home. Pope Stephen did not believe that the Lombards would keep their word, but how to get Pepin back was the question. He concluded to send an appeal from higher authority, and he sent a letter to the king purporting to have been written by Saint Peter himself, and promising Pepin that if he would come at once to the rescue of the Church, he should conquer his own enemies all the rest of his life and should be sure of the joys of heaven.

After hearing this letter, the Franks were wildly eager to return to Italy. They overcame the Lombards and again shut them up in Pavia. This time the Lombards were thoroughly subdued. They had taken a number of walled towns, and these Pepin had recaptured. He now made Pope Stephen a present, namely, the keys of the gates of all these cities. This was the beginning of the owning of territory by the Popes.

Under Charles Martel Europe was saved from the Mohammedans. Under Pepin, the power of the Church was greatly strengthened. The rule of these two men lasted only a little more than half a century, but in this time they accomplished more than the whole line of the Do-Nothing kings.

CHAPTER VII

CHARLEMAGNE AND HIS KINGDOM

CHARLES, the prince who when a boy of twelve had been sent to receive the Pope, became king at the death of Pepin, and a real king he was. He accomplished so much in his reign that he is known in history as "Charles the Great," or "Charlemagne." There was no hint of the Do-Nothings about this ruler. He was one of the most energetic men who ever lived; and if ever a king needed energy, he did.

Of course, like all other rulers of the time, he had to do a great deal of fighting. During thirty of the forty-six years of his reign he was continually sending expeditions against the Saxons, who lived at the north, just across the Rhine. Both Franks and Saxons were of the Teutonic race, but each despised the other. "You Franks have given up the free life of the forest and have built yourselves cities," said the Saxons scornfully; "you have taken one Christ for your God, and have given up Thor who wields the thunderbolts." And the Franks retorted, "You Saxons are only savages and heathen." "Cæsar with all the power of Rome could not conquer us," declared the Saxons proudly, "and in the depths of our wilderness there stands a pillar in memory of the day when the legions of the Roman Varus were cut down like grass."

Such were the people whom Charlemagne meant

to overcome, for, large as his kingdom was, he aimed at making it still larger. He fought his way into the forest until he came to the place that every Saxon held sacred, for here stood the column in honor of the Roman defeat. There was also a fortress. Charlemagne took the fortress and broke up the column, and also the altar on which the Saxons used to sacrifice human beings to the god Thor. He even cut down the sacred oak trees that grew around the altar; and now at last the Saxons owned defeat and agreed to pay him tribute.

Charlemagne was, according to the ideas of his day, an earnest missionary. Wherever he went, he built not only strong castles, but also churches, and he sent preachers as well as soldiers. In spite of their promises, the Saxons promptly killed the preachers and burned the churches. Then followed the stern vengeance of the Frankish king. He came down upon the Saxons, took thousands of them prisoners, and put them to death. He carried away thousands of others and scattered them over his kingdom. At last the Saxons had to yield, and their chief agreed to enter a convent. Then Charlemagne began his missionary work in earnest. "Will you be baptized or put to death?" he would ask. It is no wonder that the numbers of his converts increased rapidly. At length it occurred to him that he might accomplish still more by bribery. "Whoever comes of his own will to baptism shall receive a fine white tunic," he declared; and now they came — not once, but many times!

Aquitania revolted, but Charlemagne subdued the revolt, and at the same time skillfully overcame the strongest objections of the Aquitanians to his rule, for he gave them his baby son for a king. The little sovereign was carried part way in a cradle; but his escort thought that he ought to enter his kingdom in a more dignified fashion, so they dressed him in a little suit of armor and gave him a tiny sword. Then they put him on a horse and carefully held him there, and he entered in all the glory of a warrior bold.

Five years before the Aquitanian war came to an end, the Pope again appealed for help against the troublesome Lombards. Charlemagne crossed the Alps, and now the Lombard king was put into a monastery, and his son fled to Constantinople. Charlemagne had hardly reached home before the Pope sent a second appeal: The Lombards were revolting, would he come again? He came, he subdued them, and he made a second young prince, a boy of four years, King of Italy.

The next appeal to Charlemagne came from the Mohammedans, or Moors, in northern Spain. "We can no longer submit to the Caliph of Cordova," they declared. "If you will come and help us against him, we will become your faithful subjects." Of course Charlemagne could not say no to such a tempting invitation, and he marched with an army straight across the Pyrenees and into Spain. He took a few cities, and then he marched home again, just why is not known. The rear guard and the bag-

CHARLEMAGNE IMPOSING BAPTISM ON THE SAXONS

gage were in charge of Roland, nephew of the king and "Lord of the Breton March," that is, governor of the borderland of Francia, next to Brittany. In going through the narrow pass of Roncesvalles in the Pyrenees, he was set upon by the enemy and not a man survived. Because of this expedition, Charlemagne claimed that portion of Spain lying south of the Pyrenees as a part of his kingdom, but he never ceased to mourn for his valiant nephew and follower.

Charlemagne's vast kingdom was made up of many different peoples, and each had its own kind of government. Some had written laws, some had only customs that had been handed down, and some had hardly anything that could be called government. It was not an easy thing to bring under the same laws all these peoples with their different ways of living and thinking, but this was what Charlemagne aimed at doing. Twice every year he called together the chief men of the kingdom. The more important of these two meetings was held in May, and was called the "Field of May."

In good weather the people who came to the Field of May assembled out of doors. There must have been great crowds, and the king moved about among his subjects with a friendly word for each. Leading men from the different parts of the country were asked to inform him of the condition of the people near their homes, whether they were contented or restless, whether there was any disorder, and if so, what its cause might be. Those who were to consider any new laws that he might propose withdrew by themselves to discuss matters. If they wished to ask any questions, they sent a messenger to the king; or, if they preferred, he would come to them and talk things over in most familiar fashion. When these men had come to an agreement, they reported it to the king, and he made the final decision.

To make sure that these laws were carried out, Charlemagne gave each district into the charge of some officer, or "count"; and to find out whether these officers did their duty, he sent out superior officers, whom people called the "Emperor's Eyes." They traveled from one district to another, looking everywhere to ascertain not only whether the laws were obeyed, but whether the people were treated fairly. If any count was unjust, they quietly settled themselves in his house to keep watch of him. He had to pay for their support, and in order to get rid of them, he usually reformed very promptly.

Charlemagne had a vast respect for learned men. It is said that two strangers once came to his court, saying that they had brought wisdom to sell. "What is your price?" asked the king. "Food and clothes, a room for a school, and pupils willing to learn," they replied. Charlemagne was soon obliged to leave for war, but before he went he gave into the charge of the learned men some boys of poor parents and some who were sons of nobles. When he came home, he commanded the boys to show him what they had learned. The poor boys had done well, but the young noblemen had trusted that the wealth and rank of their fathers would give them success in life, and they had done very little. The king praised the poor boys. "Keep on as you have begun," he said, "and you shall ever be honored in my eyes." Then he turned upon the rich boys and thundered: "You have idled and gambled and trusted in your wealth, and you have disobeyed my orders. Understand that if you do not make up for this by hard work, you will never get anything from Charles."

A really great man is always glad to gather great men around him, and this Charlemagne was always eager to do. Nearly all the famous scholars of the time were induced by him to come to his court. Some of them he sent to Italy and Aquitania to advise his sons in their government. Some he sent out as commissioners to other parts of his kingdom. Some he kept at his own palace. They taught his children, and they also held a school for the grown folk, a sort of conference where many subjects were discussed. It was much the fashion to choose for one's self and use among one's friends some name from history or literature, and in this palace school each one had a special name. The king called himself David; his sister Gisela became Lucia, his daughter Gisela was Delia. One of his courtiers took the name of Nathanael; another that of Homer. In science it was not the custom to study nature, but to accept any fancy that occurred to the teacher. When Alcuin taught arithmetic, for instance, he declared that the numbers 3 and 6 contained "the keys of nature" — whatever that may mean. When the planet Mars disappeared from the sky, Charlemagne asked Alcuin why this occurred; and Alcuin replied that the sun had delayed the planet. He asked why a comet had appeared, and was told that it was the soul of a man who had recently died. Alcuin often had rather a hard time, for Charlemagne was not only eager to learn, but he had an excellent memory; and when the teacher explained some marvel of nature by one fancy, and a little later by another fancy, the king was quite likely to ask how the two statements could both be true. Long after poor Alcuin had left court and retired to an abbey at Tours, he spoke of some of his mistakes and said that they ought to be overlooked. "The horse," he said, "which has four legs often stumbles; how much more must man, who has but one tongue, often trip in speech." Alcuin wrote Latin poetry, and the following is a translation of one of his poems:

"*Spring*. I am fain for the cuckoo's coming, the bird that I love the best;
And there's not a roof where the cuckoo deigns to pause in his flight and rest,
And pipe glad songs from his ruddy beak, but will call him a welcome guest.

"*Winter*. Delay me the coming of cuckoo! The father of toils is he;
And battles he brings, and all men in the world, however weary they be,
Must rouse them from rest at his trumpet to brave land-farings and perils at sea.

"*Spring*. The note of the cuckoo brings flowers and gladdens with honey the bee,
Sends the landsman to build up his homestead, the ship to the unruffled sea,
And the nestlings are hatched by his music, and the meadow glows green and the tree."

Next to Alcuin, Charlemagne was the most learned man in the kingdom. He spoke Latin readily and understood Greek. He studied grammar and rhetoric; he was interested in art and music and especially in astronomy. Penmanship he found difficult, for his hand was more used to holding a sword than a stylus, the pointed instrument used in writing on waxen tablets. He kept such tablets and a stylus under his pillow so he could practice when wakeful; but he never learned to write a good hand.

When the year 800 had come, Charlemagne was at Rome hearing mass, which was celebrated by the Pope himself. Whether Charlemagne knew what was coming or not, no one can say, but suddenly the Pope turned to where the king knelt before the altar, placed a crown upon his head, and anointed him with the holy oil. The crowd, probably instructed beforehand, cried, in the ancient form of words used in accepting an emperor, "To Charles Augustus, crowned of God, great and peaceful Emperor of the Romans, life and victory!" The Roman Empire, once so powerful, had been divided long before this, and the western part had not had an emperor for more than three hundred years. In crowning Charlemagne, then, the Pope was reviving the old title, and declaring him to be "Emperor of the Romans," and at the head of what came to be called the "Holy Roman Empire," though, as has been often said, it was "neither holy, nor Roman, nor an empire."

Charlemagne died in 814. Several years before his death, he made his will with the utmost care, dividing his property among his children, the poor, his servants, and the Church. He called the chief men of the empire together and "invited" them to make his son Louis emperor. They agreed willingly. Immediately after this, father and son met them in the cathedral at Aix-la-Chapelle. Charlemagne, in his kingly robes and with his crown on his head, first knelt in prayer, then, standing facing his son, he addressed him on the duties of a sovereign to the Church and the people. "Are you fully resolved to fulfill these duties?" he asked solemnly. "I am," replied Louis. The king had laid a second crown up upon the altar, and he said, "Take the crown from the altar and place it upon your head." Louis did this, and all the people shouted, "Long live the Emperor Louis!" Charlemagne then formally declared that his son would rule together with him, and with the prayer, "Blessed be Thou, O Lord God, who hast granted me grace to see with mine own eyes my son seated on my throne!" the ceremony came to an end.

Charlemagne gave strict commands about the manner of his burial. In obedience to these, his body was placed in a little stone chapel. He was seated in a chair or throne, a gold chain about his neck and a scepter in his right hand. A Bible lay open on his knees, and a sword hung at his side. In one of the laments on his death there was written, "Many are the afflictions that Frankland has known, but never knew she such a sorrow as when at Aachen she laid in the earth the august and eloquent Charles."

CHAPTER VIII

THE SONG OF ROLAND

ROLAND, who fell at Roncesvalles, was Charlemagne's nephew and one of the bravest of knights. This is all that is really known of him, but that is enough for a legend. There was something so touching about the early death of the gallant young Roland that people told the story over and over. They put in what details they knew and added others that they imagined. Minstrels sang songs of Roncesvalles, and by and by some poet, no one knows his name, put the story into the form of a poem, and in this form it has been handed down to us for eight hundred years.

Of course the poet who wrote this "Song of Roland" was more interested in making a poem than in being historically accurate, and he begins the story by saying that Charlemagne had been in Spain seven years, winning victories wherever he went. Saragossa was the only city not yet conquered. Its king, Marsila, realizing that he could not resist the great emperor, sent messengers to ask for peace.

The ten envoys, dressed in the richest of robes and riding upon the whitest of mules, set out for the camp of Charlemagne. In their hands they carried branches of olive. Four hundred mules followed them, laden with silver and gold. "We will be baptized," the envoys were to say, "and we will give our sons to you as hostages. We will agree to hold fair Spain as a fief of yours, if you and your army will but cross the Pyrenees and return to the land of the Franks."

Then Charlemagne and his barons discussed the offer of Marsila. Roland sprang to his feet. "Do you not remember," he cried, "that once before this same Marsila sent you an olive branch, but that when you accepted his submission and sent envoys to him in return, he slew them falsely and treacherously? O my king, let us carry on the war in the good old fashion, the fashion that has no failure for its end! Let us storm the walls of Saragossa and conquer this maker of false promises!"

Then arose Ganelon, stepfather of Roland, and urged the emperor to accept the submission of Marsila. So advised others, and then the question arose, Who is to go? Roland begged to be sent, but Charlemagne refused. Then Roland named Ganelon, and Ganelon was sent, in a mad rage and vowing revenge upon his stepson.

Once arrived at the court of Marsila, he delivered the message of Charlemagne nobly and as a faithful knight of the great emperor should do. Then his hatred of Roland overcame him, and for the sake of vengeance he was ready to betray his stepson and his sovereign.

"King Marsila," said the faithless envoy, "with all your power you could never overcome Charlemagne in open battle, but by craft and artful cunning you may do more than you dream. Listen to what I would advise. Do you send costly gifts and the keys of your city and many hostages to Charlemagne in proof that you have yielded to him. He will start for home happy and unsuspecting. Then, when he is far ahead, do you come upon the rear guard and cut them down to a man. Never will Charlemagne recover from such a blow, and never again will he venture to cross the Pyrenees or disturb you in your kingdom."

"Do you swear by all that is holy to keep faith with me?" demanded Marsila. "I swear it," declared the traitor, "and what is more, I swear that the leader of the rear guard shall be one Roland, nephew of Charlemagne and dearest to his heart."

So the evil plan was formed, and Ganelon set out on his return, with seven hundred camels loaded with gold and silver for Charlemagne, and the richest gifts for the traitor who was plotting to work his overthrow.

Charlemagne and his knights were watching anxiously; and when Ganelon came in sight and told them that all was well, that Marsila yielded and sent gifts and hostages and the keys of Saragossa, they were overjoyed, and could hardly plan rewards generous enough to repay the successful envoy.

Straightway the camp was broken up and the army made ready to set out on the march to Francia and home, to their wives and their children. Charlemagne did not suspect any treachery, but he was a careful general, and he planned that, while the main part of his army was marching over the mountains, a faithful body of men should be left as rear guard to make their safety sure. To lead this rear guard was a post of danger, but it was also a post of honor, and when the traitor Ganelon suggested that Roland should be in command, the other knights rejoiced that the gallant young warrior was to have this recognition of his bravery.

With trumpets and banners Charlemagne and his followers started on their homeward way. Roland put on his well-polished armor, buckled on his beloved sword Durendal, his trusty sword with the golden hilt, mounted his noble horse Veillantif, and waved the white banner fastened to the end of his lance. Oliver, his dearest friend, whose sister was his betrothed, galloped to his side, and soon the line was formed. The emperor and his hundred thousand followers waved their banners in farewell and marched slowly up the mountain ridges. With the passing of every hour, home was nearer, and they were more and more happy — all but the emperor. For him, too, wife and children were waiting, but he feared for his beloved Roland and the rear guard. He remembered that Ganelon had named him for the place of danger, and he recalled the look of hatred in Ganelon's eyes as he spoke the name of his stepson. Then, too, Charlemagne had had a dream wherein he had seen great evil befall the brave young knight. But such fancies as these were no reason for turning back with his army, and though sad and gloomy, he marched on away from Spain and Roland.

The emperor might well have had visions of evil befalling Roland, for four hundred thousand of the pagans were advancing upon him. There were but twenty thousand of the rear guard, for in spite of Charlemagne's urging, Roland had scorned to take more. The music of Saracen clarions and the heavy tramping of Saracen feet could be heard, and Oliver begged Roland to sound a blast on his horn that the emperor might hear it and come to their aid; but Roland was fired with the thought of the glory that he and his little troop might win, and he refused. Again and yet again did Oliver beg him to blow his horn, but Roland would not yield, and soon the mighty forces of the pagans were upon them.

The poet does not hesitate to make a story thrilling while he is about it. Oliver kills seven hundred with the broken fragment of a lance. All but one man of the ten thousand in the advance guard of the Saracens soon fall, and that one man flees for his life. But other pagan thousands were coming, and at last Roland sounded his horn. Thirty leagues away Charlemagne heard it and knew that it was the horn of Roland, and that he was in dire distress. A second time it sounded and even a third, but fainter and fainter. Then Charlemagne and his men put spurs to their horses and dashed back toward the pass of Roncesvalles, where Roland and his little band of fifty were doing their best to meet sixty thousand of their enemies. Oliver fell, and before long only Roland and Archbishop Turpin, the fighting archbishop, were alive. Four hundred pagans had banded to-

ROLAND AT RONCESVALLES

gether to kill Roland; but when they heard the distant trumpets of the emperor, they fled in rage and terror.

The archbishop was sorely wounded, but with his last breath he pronounced a blessing upon the brave twenty thousand who had fallen in the battle. Roland was faint from loss of blood and knew that his hour had come. He threw himself down under a great pine tree to die with his face toward Spain. "Here my emperor shall find me, with face to the foe, as a conqueror should lie," he said to himself; and then he prayed, "Father, O Father, forgive me my sins and grant me to live with Thee in Thy heaven!"

Under the pine tree the emperor found his beloved knight, and fell by his side, fainting with grief. But the foes of the Franks were upon him, an enormous army brought together from forty kingdoms. They were routed, Saragossa fell into the hands of Charlemagne, and its inhabitants had to choose between the sword and the waters of baptism. The sister of Oliver fell dead on hearing the news of the death of her betrothed and her brother. Ganelon met with a terrible punishment; and so the story ends.

CHAPTER IX

HOW THE NORTHMEN BECAME NORMANS

ONCE upon a time Charlemagne was in a little seashore town of Francia on the borders of the Mediterranean. As he and his followers sat at the table eating dinner, they caught sight of a fleet of vessels coming into port. "Those are Jewish traders," declared some of the company; but others thought they came from Africa, and one or two questioned whether they were not British. "No," said Charlemagne, "those are not traders; see how lightly they are built. They are made to carry men, not goods, and they are laden with the cruelest of our foes, the barbarous Northmen."

Then the Franks ran swiftly to their ships to drive away the pirates. They might just as well have saved their strength and finished their dinner, for in some way the Northmen learned that the great emperor was there, and they slipped away into the mist as fast as sails and oars would carry them.

Charlemagne did not return to the table, but stood by the window a long while, gazing in the direction whence the vessels had disappeared. Tears were in his eyes as he turned toward his followers and said, "I have no fear of any harm coming to me from those miserable pirates, but I grieve to think what evils they will heap upon my children and my poor people in the years that are to come."

These Northmen were wild marauders from Scandinavia, who had no fear of the maddest tempest, but dashed out into the stormy seas, landing at dead of night wherever the wind chanced to drive them, burning crops and houses and murdering the people. Britain and Ireland had already endured much from them, and Francia, as Charlemagne foretold, was also to suffer from their ravages.

After the death of Charlemagne there was no one of his family — or of any other family, for that matter — strong enough to rule his enormous empire. It was divided and subdivided; and there was dissension and war; but at length, in 843, a treaty was made at Verdun by which his lands were divided into three broad strips and given to his three grandsons respectively. Roughly speaking, the most western strip became France; the middle strip included Italy, the valley of the Rhone, and a belt of land extending to the mouth of the Rhine; the most eastern strip became Germany. This was the first great treaty among the European states.

Meanwhile the Northmen were becoming more and more daring. They glided up the rivers of Francia far into the country. Sometimes they besieged a city, sometimes a traitor let them within its walls. The monasteries and churches were full of treasures, and so these were the special aim of the pirates. The abbot of Saint Denis was carried away and made to pay a heavy ransom. Worst of all, sometimes a king would agree with the Northmen that if they would leave his own lands untouched, he would not interfere with their pillage of his subjects. To one of these kings the Archbishop of Rheims wrote indignantly on hearing that he made no effort to defend his people.

In 885, the Northmen, under one Siegfried, pushed up the Seine to Paris. They had expected to capture the city without any difficulty, and they were amazed to see new towers and ramparts and a strong double wall. Siegfried landed alone and demanded to speak with Bishop Gozlin, governor of the city. "All we want is to go farther up the river," he said, "and if you will allow us to pass the city, we will harm neither person nor property." "I do not believe your story," declared the bishop, "and I will give you no such passage." "Then shall our armies launch their poisoned arrows against you, and you shall be given over to all the horrors of famine." But the bishop stood firm, and Siegfried went back to his ships, vowing vengeance.

For thirteen long months the siege went on. The Northmen made great wheeled sheds, each one concealing a battering ram. They made smaller sheds covered with hides to protect men from fire while they were trying to breach the walls. They did their best to fill the fosse by throwing in earth, leaves, branches of trees, and even bodies of their prisoners, slain for the purpose. The defenders responded with crossbows and machines for throwing stones and with long beams with iron points; but now came a new terror, for the Northmen had driven three burning ships near to the city walls. But the ships struck on the stone piers of the bridge, and the walls stood.

So the months passed. The bishop died and the Northmen took new courage. The brave Count Odo was now left in command of the Franks, and he forced his way through the ranks of his foes to appeal to the king for aid. But the king was made of different stuff. He dawdled and delayed, and when he finally came to the help of his city, all he did was to tell the Northmen that if they would leave Paris alone, they were welcome to go up the river and plunder Burgundy as much as they chose. He even added to this permission a bribe of seven hundred pounds of silver. Such was the king who reigned over men like Bishop Gozlin and Count Odo.

When Siegfried advanced upon Paris, Rollo, one of the leaders of the Northmen, was sent to take possession of Rouen. This he did, and, much to the surprise of its people, he treated them kindly, was careful not to injure their buildings, and even repaired their city walls. Here was a viking who was actually somewhat respectable. Indeed, it was said that he had visited England more than once, not as a robber, but as a guest of King Alfred the Great and his successor. He was becoming so powerful that the wisest course was to make friends with him. The king consulted with his councilors, and soon the Archbishop of Rouen was sent to the Northmen with an important offer. This said in brief: "If you will acknowledge yourself to be my vassal [that is, do military service when needed], and will agree to be baptized as a Christian, I will give you land and also the hand of my daughter Gisela in marriage."

Rollo and his comrades talked the matter over. As far as land was concerned, they held a large territory already, and they could win more whenever they chose, for people much preferred having them as settlers and neighbors to enduring the terrible sufferings inflicted by their raids. On the other hand, Rollo was beginning to see that piracy was not the most desirable kind of life. He really had an inclination to rule a country justly and fairly, rather than to be ever robbing and murdering. He agreed that a day should be appointed to discuss terms of peace.

When the day came, the king took his stand on one shore of a little river, while Rollo and his followers stood on the opposite bank. Messages were carried back and forth. "I will grant you Flanders," said the king. "That is too swampy," objected Rollo. "Then I will give you the maritime part of Normandy." "That is nothing but forests," Rollo declared; and the king did not venture to retort that the cultivated fields had been laid waste by the raids of the Northmen. Finally, land was agreed upon, and the Duchy of Normandy was formed.

Rollo was not fully instructed in the manners of royal circles, and when the bishops told him that in acknowledgment of such a gift he should kiss the foot of the king, he stoutly refused. "I bend my knee to no man," he declared, "and I kiss the foot of none." The bishops urged that it was only a form, but that it was quite proper and necessary. "Do it for me, then," Rollo commanded one of his comrades. The warrior bold had no more intention of kneeling than his master. Bolt upright he stood and raised the foot of the astounded king to his lips. Naturally the king toppled over, and the throng shouted with amusement. The king and all his nobles, dukes, counts, and abbots swore solemnly to protect Rollo in his possession of the land. He was baptized by the French name of Robert, and so the wild Northern pirate became ruler of Rouen and much country thereabouts.

Rollo now had land of his own to defend, and he set to work to cultivate it and to care for his people as energetically as he had carried on his earlier career of robbery. The manners of the wild rovers became more civilized. Their very names were softened for "Northmen" became "Normans," and "Rollo," also called "Rolf" or "Hroth," became "Rou." For twenty years he governed his broad domain. He rebuilt the towns which his countrymen had destroyed, he befriended the Church, and he treated his people justly. Wrongdoing he punished with a heavy hand. Whoever was injured by another had the right to shout "Haro!" and every one within hearing was bound to join in the chase for the culprit. A legend says that in order to find out whether his laws were observed, Rollo hung his golden bracelet upon the branch of a tree, and that when he went to look for it three years later, he found it still hanging there. This might be a little easier to believe if the same story had not been told of Alfred the Great and other wise rulers.

Whether there is any truth in this legend of the bracelet or not, it is certain that before long the Normans had become more French than the Franks themselves. Within forty years after the founding of Rollo's duchy, French manners and customs prevailed, and French was more generally spoken in Normandy than the old tongue of the Northmen. These sea rovers had a remarkable aptitude for adopting the best of the ways of other folk and improving upon them; and before much time had passed, the Normans became leaders in building, in commerce, and even in literature.

CHAPTER X

HOW A NORMAN BECAME KING OF ENGLAND

One of the earliest memories of William of Normandy was of being dressed handsomely and led into the castle hall, where he found his father and a number of other men. The boy heard his father say: "This is my son. He is little, but he will grow." Then these men, one by one, knelt before the boy, laid their hands in his, and promised to be faithful to him. He was only seven or eight years old, but he understood the meaning of this ceremony, namely, that they were now bound to fight for him if he called upon them.

The father of the child was Robert, Duke of Normandy, one of the successors of Rollo the Northman. Some of the Normans called the duke "Robert the Devil." More than one crime was laid to his charge, but, according to the belief of the day, these would all be forgiven if he only made a pilgrimage to Jerusalem; and this he was about to do. Robert died on the journey, and the boy became Duke of Normandy.

Those were stormy times in Normandy. Many a man would not have hesitated a moment to kill the child in the hope of getting possession of his inheritance, and among them were some of the very nobles who had sworn to be faithful to him. Others realized what horrors of warfare the death of this boy would bring upon the duchy, and they guarded him with their lives. He could never be left alone a moment for fear of poison or assassination. Sometimes he was caught up in the night and carried from one castle to another. Sometimes he was hidden away for safety in the cottage of his grandfather; for his mother was the daughter of a peasant. The King of France, to whom he paid homage for his duchy, had promised in return to protect him; but the king was beginning to be jealous of the strength of Normandy. He did not realize, however, how powerful it was, and after William became a man, the king swept into the duchy with his forces, expecting to conquer it at a dash. On the contrary, he was driven from the land so promptly that he was only too glad to make peace.

William was able also to make his peace with the Pope. The duke had married Matilda of Flanders, although for some reason that is not clearly understood the Pope had objected. He was after some years persuaded to confirm the marriage on condition that William and Matilda would build four hospitals, one in each of the four chief towns of Normandy, and also one convent for men and one for women.

Life was now moving more easily for William, but his greatest adventure still lay before him. This is the way it came about. A few years before William was born, his great aunt and her husband were driven from the English throne and with their two little boys fled to Normandy. Edward, the elder of the two boys, was twenty-five years older than the young duke, and he promised William that if he ever became King of England, he would bequeath him the English crown. It did not seem to enter his mind that the English people might have a word to say about the matter.

William never forgot this promise of King Edward, and he watched every movement of the people across the English Channel. One of the most prominent of these people was Earl Harold, son of a powerful noble. Edward had at last begun to suspect that the English would not accept a foreigner as king, and his thoughts, as well as the wishes of the English people, turned toward Harold. William had learned this, and when one day Harold went out sailing and a storm drove his boat upon the coast of Normandy, William's mind was made up just what course to follow.

Day after day passed in royal entertainment for the visitor, with feasts, games, hunting, hawking, even a choice bit of warfare, for William invited his guest to help him subdue a disobedient vassal. On the way home from this amusement, they were riding along side by side when William began to talk of the days when King Edward lived at his father's castle. "He was like an older brother to me," said the duke, "and he promised to bequeath me his crown if he should ever become King of England. There may be difficulties in the way, and if you will promise me your aid, I promise in return to do for you whatever you may ask of me."

Harold well knew that if he refused he would probably be thrown into one of the dungeons in William's castle, and he made the promise. A few days later, William invited him to come to an assembly of the barons. A table covered with cloth of gold stood before the duke. On it were two reliquaries, or caskets holding relics of the saints. "Harold," said William, "you have already promised to aid me in gaining the throne of England. I ask you now to swear to this on these relics of the saints and in the presence of my barons." Harold laid his hands on the two reliquaries and took the oath. To swear on the bones of the less important saints was looked upon as a sin, of course, but a sin for which one might by doing penance win forgiveness, and probably Harold had no idea of keeping his promise; but suddenly the cloth of gold was removed, and he was aghast to see that he had sworn on a great tub full to the brim of the most sacred relics of the Church in Normandy.

Early in 1066 King Edward died, and Harold was made king. William at once sent a swift messenger to say to him, "William, Duke of Normandy, recalls to you the oath that you swore to him on the relics of the saints." Harold replied: "An oath sworn under compulsion is not binding. Moreover, the kingship belongs not to me, but to the country. I cannot put it from me without the country's consent."

Then began mighty preparations for conquest. Many hundred vessels were brought together at the mouth of the Dive River, and many thousand men crossed the Channel. The battle which followed was called the battle of Hastings, because it was fought seven miles from Hastings. The Normans marched on toward the hill of Senlac, where the English were drawn up. There were slingers and archers in the Norman lines. There were the heavy-armed infantry; there were knights with sword and lance. There was even a warlike bishop, William's half-brother. The Church forbade him to use sword or spear for the shedding of blood, but he persuaded himself that it was not unlawful to swing a club. The duke himself bore neither lance nor javelin, but a heavy iron mace, a terrible weapon in the hands of so powerful a man.

Suddenly a rider galloped out in front of the Norman line, Taillefer, the minstrel. "My lord," he said to William, "I have served you long. Reward me this day for my services. Grant me to strike the first blow in the battle." "I grant it!" cried William. Then the minstrel sang the old ballads of Roland at Roncesvalles. He tossed his sword into the air and caught it as it fell. He made his horse curvet and caracole. Wheeling about, he galloped up to the lines of the English, thrust his lance through one man, cut down another with his sword, and in another moment himself lay dead, struck down by many an English weapon.

This was the beginning of a battle which made William of Normandy King of England. It was also the beginning of the holding of English land by

French dukes, and of French land by English sovereigns. Of course this was bound to make trouble between the two countries, and it was five hundred years before England was forced to surrender the last bit of her French possessions.

CHAPTER XI

HOW NORMANDY BECAME A PART OF FRANCE

Some twenty years after the great adventure of William the Norman, or William the Conqueror, as he came to be called, a strange figure was seen in France, going about from one place to another. He wore a woolen tunic and over it a rough serge cloak which reached to his heels. He was bareheaded and barefooted, and as he rode along on the back of a rather forlorn-looking mule, he stretched out one bare arm before him, carrying a crucifix in his hand. Wherever he stopped, the people gathered about him, and he preached to them in simple, homely words which, nevertheless, were eloquent and moved them wonderfully. They followed him in crowds. They treasured hairs from his mule to keep as precious relics. They brought their quarrels to him and yielded to his decisions. They loaded him with gifts — which he gave away to the first person whom he saw in need.

This strange, eloquent man was Peter the Hermit. He, as well as Robert of Normandy and thousands of others, had been on pilgrimage to Jerusalem. The Holy City had long been in the hands of the Turks, but pilgrims had been permitted to pass within its gates on payment of a tax. Another race of Turks, however, had captured Jerusalem, and now Christian pilgrims were not only obliged to pay large taxes, but they were robbed and tortured and often murdered. This was the story told by Peter the Hermit, and he begged his hearers to free the Holy Land from the infidels.

Pope Urban II had met Peter and believed in him and his message, and in a great meeting held on the plain of Clermont in France, Urban urged the thousands of people before him to put on their breasts or shoulders the red cross that was to be the sign of their vow to rescue the city of their Lord. He bade none but strong men go on the crusade, but the vast company that set out was a strange medley of men, women, and children, of good people and bad people — thieves, drunkards, and all sorts of rascals. Better soldiers soon followed them, and Jerusalem was taken. It remained in the hands of the Christians less than a century, then fell again into those of the Turks. One of the crusades undertaken in hope of recovering it might well have been called the royal crusade or the crusade of the kings, for it was led by King Philip Augustus of France and Richard the Lion-Hearted of England.

When Philip was only fifteen, his father became very ill, and, as in the case of Charlemagne, he wished to see his son crowned before his death. So all the princes and nobles hastened to Rheims, and in the great cathedral the crown was placed upon the boy's head. His father died a few months later, and Philip was left to rule alone. He was an ambitious young king, and his great dream was to make his kingdom as large as it had been in the days of

Charlemagne. There was not much prospect of this coming true, and of course Philip knew it; but he had another dream not quite so ambitious, namely, that some day he would make Normandy a part of the kingdom of France, and this was not at all impossible.

Into the midst of Philip's dreams the news came that the Turks had captured the Holy City. All Europe was bewailing its loss. No king could hope to be honored by his people who did not do his best to help recover Jerusalem. Men were half wild to go on a crusade, and those who could not go submitted willingly to a tax amounting to one tenth of their property in order to pay the expenses of an expedition. Philip and Richard started for the Holy Land. Each wanted to be the hero of the crusade, and as the glory was inclined to fall into the hands of Richard, Philip was not at all pleased, and before long he set out on his return to France.

Besides his jealousy, Philip had another reason for hastening home. He had made a solemn promise not to touch Richard's land or to injure him in any way while he was on the crusade. To break such a promise would be a serious matter and would get Philip into trouble, not only with English and Normans and even some of his own people, but also with the Church. If, however, he could persuade the Pope to release him from the promise, he could seize the land before Richard could get home — and this land was the coveted Normandy.

But the Pope refused to have anything to do with

such a trick, and Philip set to work to form new plans. His first step was to make a bargain with John, Richard's younger brother. Philip was to help John get possession of the English throne, and in return John was to agree not to interfere with Philip's seizing Normandy. All was going on smoothly for the treacherous plotters when news came that Richard had made a truce with the Turks which would permit pilgrims to visit Jerusalem in peace, and was already on his way home. A little later they learned that he had been shipwrecked and was now in the hands of the Emperor of Germany. This suited them to perfection, and they offered the emperor a large sum of money if he would hold on to his captive. Possibly the emperor guessed what the plotters were about and did not care to increase the power of France; but, however that may be, he accepted the offer of the English people to pay a huge ransom for their crusader king and set Richard free. "Beware, the devil is unchained," wrote Philip to John.

Richard was never revengeful, and he forgave his brother. Then he set out to try to protect Normandy, but he was slain, and John was now King of England and Duke of Normandy, although Normandy — and England too for that matter — belonged to his young nephew Arthur.

The people of Normandy did not like John, and Philip found them more than willing to accept Arthur for their duke. But Arthur fell into his uncle's hands and was put into prison. One day the door of his room was thrown open and King John entered. He spoke to the boy pleasantly and asked him if he would like to have a row on the Seine River. Of course he was delighted, and they got into the boat. When they had come to a lonely place, King John suddenly drew his sword, turned upon his nephew, and stabbed him to the heart. This is the story that was generally believed, and, at any rate, Arthur was never seen again.

John was now King of England, to be sure, but he was also Duke of Normandy, and as duke he was a vassal of Philip and must obey him if he wished to keep the Norman lands. Philip summoned him to come for trial on the charge of having murdered his nephew. He paid no attention to the summons, and Philip — not at all unwillingly — declared his lands forfeited. So it was that Normandy became a part of the kingdom of France.

CHAPTER XII

THE KING WHO WAS A SAINT

WHEN Prince Louis was only twelve years old, the death of his father made him King Louis IX. Fortunately for the boy, his mother, Queen Blanche, was a very wise woman. She knew that the barons would be likely to refuse to support her son, but they were scattered over the kingdom, and before they could come together and make any definite plots, she had him firmly seated on the throne and the government going on in his name.

Within two weeks after the funeral of his father, Louis was made a knight. There was a long ceremony, of course, but on the same day the court moved to Rheims for the coronation; and that night the young king kept vigil before the altar in the great lonely cathedral. On the following day, although he must have been a very tired and sleepy boy, he walked up to the altar barefooted before a great company of knights, bishops, peers, and peeresses, and there took a solemn oath to be faithful to God and the Church, and to deal justly with his people. He was anointed with the holy oil, the royal scepter of power was placed in his right hand, and the small rod of mercy in his left, and then the crown of France was laid upon his head.

Louis was King of France, and everything was done in his name, but the queen was the real ruler

SAINT LOUIS OPENING THE PRISONS OF HIS REALM

and guardian of her son. In those days people believed that children should be brought up with the greatest severity, and although Queen Blanche loved her son with all her heart, she would have thought herself a weak and foolish woman if she had not treated him with sternness. When he was fourteen, she put him into the hands of a tutor who believed that the upright, obedient boy ought to be whipped every day because it would be good discipline for him. Kings cannot run away, so the boy had to bear it as best he could, and somehow he never lost his kind, gentle disposition and his love of making the people around him happy.

Queen Blanche ruled the land wisely and managed to subdue the turbulent barons. In spite of her strictness, Louis loved her, and even after he came of age to rule by himself, he always set the highest value upon her advice. Kind and thoughtful of others as he was, he would never yield when he was sure that he was in the right. He gave careful consideration to the question whether he ought not to return Normandy to England; but when some of the French barons tried to get possession of portions of the land properly belonging to the crown, he would not give up a single inch. To his own brother he said, "Charles, there must be only one king in France."

Although Louis stood so resolutely for his rights, he was full of sympathy for all in need. With his own hands he cared for lepers too loathsome for others to touch. In remembrance of Jesus' washing the feet of his disciples, this humble sovereign washed the feet of poor beggars one day of each week. He even bore it patiently when one of the beggars found fault with him for not doing the work more thoroughly. It is no wonder that even during his lifetime he was known as "Saint Louis."

But this royal saint had a keen sense of humor, and was never at a loss for a witty reply. At festivals and on all public occasions he always dressed handsomely, but aside from this he wore such simple clothes that his wife objected. "You wish me to wear costly stuffs," he said to her; "but since the wedding law holds that the wife must please the husband and the husband the wife, you must, in your turn, be kind enough to put off all your fine attire. You conform to my ways and I to yours." When some one ventured to hint that he was giving too much time to prayer, he said, "But no one would criticize me for giving as much time to hunting or to dice; why, then, should I be blamed for spending the time in praying?"

Of course King Louis was deeply interested in the crusades, and he must have often longed earnestly but vainly to take part in them. He was never strong, and after a while the time came when he was dangerously ill. Throughout the whole land the churches were crowded with people praying for his recovery. His subjects fasted, they gave alms, they made long processions, they did everything that they hoped would win the favor of Heaven to spare the life of their beloved king; but Louis grew worse and worse. The day came when, in spite of doctors and the holiest relics of Saint Denis, the king, who had long been unconscious, was apparently dead, and one of the nurses drew a cloth over his face. Suddenly from under the cloth there came a feeble voice, "God hath brought me back from the shadow of death," and the weeping was changed to rejoicing.

It was but a little while before Louis sent for the Bishop of Paris. "Bring me the cross of a crusader," he commanded. The bishop tried his best to dissuade him, but Louis insisted, and finally the cross was laid upon his breast. After he had recovered, Queen Blanche, bishops, and courtiers all told him in what danger he would leave his kingdom if he went on a crusade. They reminded him that when he took the cross he was too feeble to be responsible for what he was doing. Louis quietly handed the cross back to the bishop. Then he said, "I lack now neither sense nor reason; I am not weak, and I am not at the point of death; and now I demand my cross back again."

Of course many knights followed his example and put on the cross, but more were needed, and to induce them to go he played a little trick upon them. It was his custom to give each of his nobles a handsome cloak at the door of the church when they came to Mass at dawn on Christmas morning. Behold, when they had come through the darkness into the candlelight of the church and knelt in prayer, every man saw on the shoulder of each of his neighbors an embroidered cross. They took the trick good-naturedly, however, and called the king a new hunter of pilgrims and fisher of men.

King and nobles made their wills, said their farewells, and set sail to cross the Mediterranean. It was a gorgeous display. The sails of the ships were of scarlet, gold, green, or purple, and the ships themselves were painted in all the colors of the rainbow. When at length they reached Egypt, the eager king sprang ashore into water breast-high, the first of the band of crusaders. "Montjoie Saint Denis!" they shouted as they pushed on against the Saracens.

So brave a beginning ought to have led to success, but there was trouble almost from the first. They were besieged by the Saracens; pestilence and starvation were upon them. The king himself was terribly ill. Thousands of the crusaders were shut into a court with a single door. Through this door they were led out one by one. "Will you become a follower of Mohammed?" was asked of each. Those who refused were beheaded on the instant. King Louis would willingly have been among the martyrs, but he was a king, and his captors could get an enormous ransom for him; surely they were not so foolish as to let harm befall him. Handsome clothes were provided, and a friar who knew both French and Arabic was allowed to attend him; but before they discovered what was going on, the earnest prisoner was trying his best to convert his jailers to Christianity by means of this interpreter. Some of the wild Saracens demanded that he should make them knights; but he steadfastly refused to give the blessing of Christ to heathen arms, even though refusing this request endangered his life. At last a treaty was made, the ransom was paid, and the king and his followers were allowed to go free. One of them reported with great glee that the Saracens had gone off with only part of the promised ransom. The king overheard this. "Go after them," he commanded, "and see to it that the amount is paid in full." Those who had not died either in battle or in prison sailed for home. The crusade was a failure.

The power of the Saracens increased. The Christians had a strip of coast land, but they were being rapidly driven from even that. "The cross is conquered. God sleeps!" was the wail that came to the king's ears. Seventeen years after his first crusade Louis prepared for a second. He was so feeble that he had to be carried in the arms of a man to church and convent to make his farewells. All knew that the king would never return, but he went away happily, less in the hope of conquest than in the longing to win his enemies for Christ. Pestilence and the hot winds of the desert overcame what little strength remained to him. By his orders sacking was spread over a bed of cinders, and there the beloved king was laid to die. "Jerusalem, Jerusalem!" he murmured. "Lord, have pity on Thy people whom I have led here. Send them to their homes in safety. Let them not fall into the hands of Thy enemies, nor let them be forced to deny Thy Holy Name."

So died Saint Louis, the blameless king, and so ended the crusades. Jerusalem remained in the hands of the Turks until, in 1917, it was captured by General Allenby of the British army.

CHAPTER XIII

THE SIX HEROES OF CALAIS

In 1328, the King of France lay hopelessly ill, and who should succeed him was a question. He had no children, but he had a sister, Isabella, and in England the crown would have been given to her. Among one branch of the ancient Franks, however, the Salians, who lived on the lower Rhine, there was a law that no woman should rule the Salic lands. Therefore, when the king died, the French gave the crown to his cousin Philip.

But in England Edward III, a shrewd, wide-awake sovereign, was watching matters closely. He was the son of Isabella, and he argued that even if a woman could not reign, her son could. The lawyers of Europe did not agree with him, but, nevertheless, he took the title of King of France and in 1337 set to work to make it valid by force of arms.

He won a great naval victory off Sluys, on the Flemish coast, and destroyed the French fleet. He ravaged Normandy, won the famous battle of Crécy, and then marched on to Calais. He settled his troops as comfortably as possible, building for them a town of wooden huts thatched with straw. These were arranged in streets, and there was also a market-place where twice a week bread, meat, cloth, and many other comforts from England were for sale.

The wealthy people of Calais had been filling their houses with provisions, but the poorer people had not been able to do this, and the governor of the place now sent them out from the city to seek homes and food wherever they might. Edward III was a stern ruler, but his heart was touched by the sight of these hungry, suffering folk. He told his men to pass them through the lines in safety, and he ordered a hearty dinner to be prepared for them. Then he gave some money to each one, and so let them go.

The French king had not forgotten the plight of Calais, and he bade every knight and every squire of his realm come with him to its aid; and before long, the watchmen on the walls of the city saw two hundred thousand men marching to their help with banners flying in the moonlight.

But even after they had come, the passes were so carefully guarded that they found no opportunity for battle. They sent envoys to Edward and asked him, in rather childlike fashion, if he would name some place for a battle. Edward replied that if the French were so eager to fight, they might have come sooner; but that he had now done so much that he expected to be master of Calais in a very short time; and in any case, he had no idea of arranging his affairs to suit their convenience. At this the King of France withdrew and disbanded his troops.

The governor of Calais, however, was of quite different mettle. He had no idea of surrender, but the people of the town had now held out for nearly a year, and they begged the governor to ask for a parley; so he mounted the battlements and made a sign that he wished to talk with envoys from the English king. Edward sent Sir Walter de Manny, a brave and honorable knight, to hold a parley with them. Of Sir Walter the governor asked that his people might be allowed to go free, leaving the city with all its wealth to King Edward.

"That will not satisfy him," replied Sir Walter. "Your obstinate defense has cost him not only money, but many lives. He is enraged, and he declares that the life of every one in this town must be given into his hands, that he may do as he pleases with it, either accept ransom or destroy it, as he will."

Then said the governor: "We have served our king as you would have served yours. We have endured much, but we will endure as much more before we will consent that the smallest boy in this town shall fare worse than the best. I beg of you to go to the king and entreat his compassion upon us."

Sir Walter reported the parley to Edward, but the king declared firmly that he would accept nothing but unconditional surrender. Then said Sir Walter: "But, my lord, the time may come when we shall be in the hands of the French, and if you put these people to death, the French will take their revenge on us. You could not under such circumstances expect us to obey you cheerfully when you order us to go to any of your castles."

Many of the other barons agreed with Sir Walter,

and at last the king said: "I am not so obstinate as to insist upon my opinion against you all. Sir Walter, go you to the governor of Calais, and say to him that the only grace he will get from me is this: If six of the chief men of Calais will come to me, bare-headed and barefooted, with ropes around their necks and the keys of the town in their hands, then shall the rest of the people have pardon, but with these six, I will do as I please."

When the governor heard these words, he went down from the battlements into the market-place and had the bell rung for the people to come together. After they had heard the hard terms, there was great weeping and wailing, but soon Eustace de Saint-Pierre, the richest citizen of the town, rose to his feet, and said: "It would be a very great pity to suffer so many people to die through famine if any means could be found to prevent it. I have such faith and trust in finding grace before God if I die to save my townsmen that I name myself as first of the six." "I will be the second," said John Daire, another man of wealth, and four others quickly followed their example.

Amid the tears and lamentations of the people, the governor led the six heroes to the city gate where Sir Walter de Manny stood waiting. "I swear to you," said the governor, "that these six citizens are the most wealthy and respected inhabitants of Calais. I beg of you, gentle sir, to beseech the king that they may not be put to death."

"I cannot answer for what the king may do with

them," replied Sir Walter sadly, "but you may be sure that I will do all in my power to save them."

When the six heroes had come before King Edward, they fell upon their knees before him and begged for mercy. All the barons and knights and squires wept at the sight, but the king, angry for what the people of Calais had made him endure, ordered them to be taken away and beheaded. Sir Walter and the others present pleaded for mercy, but the king would not yield. "Send for the executioner," was his only reply. But Queen Philippa now knelt before him and pleaded for the men. "With great danger I crossed the sea to come to you," she said, "and I have never yet asked a favor of you. I ask you now, for the sake of the Son of the Blessed Mary and for your love to me, that you will be merciful to these six men."

The king stood looking at her in silence. Then he said: "Ah, lady, I wish you had been anywhere else than here, but I cannot refuse you. Take them and do with them as you please." So the queen took the six men to her own apartments. She cast off the halters from their necks, gave them new clothes, and served them with a generous dinner. Then they were escorted back to the city gates in safety, and for the sake of the six heroes the lives of the men of Calais were spared.

This is the story of the heroes of Calais as it is told by Froissart, a French historian who spent much time talking with men who had fought in the wars and visiting the fields where great battles had taken place. Queen Philippa was especially kind to him, and he must have enjoyed writing this story of her goodness and mercy.

CHAPTER XIV

THE STORY OF JEANNE DARC

THE warfare of Edward III in France was the beginning of the English struggle for the French crown which is known as the "Hundred Years' War." It lasted from 1337 to 1453, although it was broken by occasional times of peace.

In 1422 the King of France died. His son could not be crowned, because French sovereigns were always crowned at Rheims, and Rheims, as well as the northern half of the whole country, was in the hands of the English; but he was proclaimed as Charles VII of France. The King of England was only a baby of ten months, but his guardians quite as promptly proclaimed him too as King of France.

Charles was kind-hearted, handsome, fond of a good time, and decidedly lazy. He was willing that people should fight for him, but he had no desire to lead them. There was nothing about him to arouse enthusiasm, and many of the French would have cared little if he had lost his throne. It began to look as if this would come to pass, for the English were besieging Orleans, the last stronghold of southern France. The English, however, were in reality more discouraged than they would have been willing to admit, for their friends, the Burgundians, had deserted them. Moreover, there was an old prophecy that some day a maiden would save France, and a rumor was afloat that a young girl had been sent by Heaven to raise the siege of Orleans.

This young girl was Jeanne Darc, daughter of a peasant of Domremy. She knew what war meant, for the Burgundians had sacked her little village and desecrated the church that she loved. She and her parents had had to flee for safety, and had returned to find their home in ruins. During the long hours when she was caring for her father's flocks, she grieved over these things. One sunny day, as she stood in the little garden, she heard voices and found herself in the center of a great brightness with angels around her. "I saw them as plainly as I see you," she said to her judge long afterwards. Over and over she had the same experience and heard voices bidding her raise the siege of Orleans and conduct Charles to be crowned at Rheims.

When she spoke of the voices and their bidding, her father was angry, and the village priest thought her insane. How could she, a village maiden of seventeen, get an opportunity even to see the King of France? She begged her uncle to ask the French commander in the next town to lead her to the king. "Slap the silly girl and send her home," growled the rough soldier. Then Jeanne made her way to him. "I *must* go," she said, "I must raise the siege of Orleans; no one else can do it." She pleaded so earnestly that at last he agreed to send her to the king.

The people of the town gave her a horse, a coat of mail, a lance, and a sword; and in the respectful care of an archer and a king's messenger she journeyed to Chinon, where Charles was residing. After some delay she was brought into the great hall of the castle, where three hundred knights were assembled. The king was not nearly so richly dressed as they, and he kept himself a little out of sight to see whether she would recognize him. She looked about her a moment, then went straight to him and bowed before him. He tried to make her think that he was not the king, but she said, "In God's name, it is you and none other!"

People were impressed with her power, but whether it came from God or Satan, they were uncertain, and she was taken to Poitiers to be examined by bishops and archbishop. They argued with her and questioned her for a fortnight. When after all this they demanded of her some sign of her truth, she at last lost patience. "In the name of God," she said, "I am not come to Poitiers to show signs; take me to Orleans and I will give you signs."

After many weeks she was allowed to start for Orleans with armor, sword, white banner emblazoned with lilies and a representation of God holding the world in his hand. Priests chanting, "Come, Holy Ghost, our souls inspire," followed her horse; and behind them marched ten or twelve thousand men.

When they were not far from Orleans, Jeanne sent a letter to the English, commanding them to leave the town, and declaring that if they did not obey she would soon come and make them. The English were greatly weakened by the departure of the Burgundians; but beside this, many of them were badly frightened. If Jeanne's power came from God, they were afraid to resist her; and if it came from Satan, they were equally afraid. Between the two fears she was allowed to enter the city unmolested.

The citizens were wild with joy, but naturally the officers were slow to follow the lead of the unknown country girl. The very night after her coming they made a sortie without telling her their plans. She awoke and galloped at full speed to the fighting ground. In every struggle she was in the thickest of the fight. She was severely wounded, but never did she show any sign of fear, and eight days after her coming to Orleans, the English marched away from the rescued city. It would have been good generalship to pursue them, but Jeanne was no eager general. All that she wanted was to obey the commands of her "voices"; she had nothing to do with pursuit. Her work was to conduct Charles to Rheims to be crowned, and then she would be free to return to her village home, to the simple life to which she had always been used.

But what was Charles about in those stirring days? He was in a castle on the banks of the Loire River, amusing himself. The very day after Orleans was free, the Maid of Orleans, as she was henceforth called, set out to find him. She rode toward him, bearing the victorious banner. Charles took off his cap and held out his hand to her. He was pleased with what she had done, but when she urged him to

JEANNE DARC AT THE CORONATION OF CHARLES VII

start at once for Rheims, he hesitated. The council said it was a long journey, and he had not the money for it. Then, too, it would be dangerous, and there were no troops ready.

After a month of delay, they set forth. When they came to the town of Troyes, which was held by the English, Charles and his council were ready to give up; but Jeanne made such energetic preparations for an assault that the citizens were alarmed and threw open their gates. The king was conducted to Rheims, and in the cathedral he was crowned by the archbishop, while Jeanne stood joyfully by, holding the royal standard.

When Charles asked her to name her reward, she would have nothing for herself, but begged that Domremy might be free from taxation. Charles promised, and for more than three centuries France kept the promise sacred. Jeanne now wished to go home. "I have done what I was bidden," she said, "and now I would gladly go back to my father and mother and care for their sheep and cattle." But Charles insisted upon her remaining to help drive the English from the northern part of the country.

Jeanne did her best, but her inspiration was gone. She had done what her "voices" commanded her to do, and they now warned her that she would be a prisoner before many months had passed. So it was. She fell into the hands of the Burgundians, who had again joined the English, and they sold her to England. The English believed that, even if she was kept in prison, her influence would prevent their success, and they tried her on the charge of witchcraft. She had given Charles a kingdom, and he did not raise his hand in her behalf. In the market-place of Rouen she was bound to a stake to die by fire. She asked for a cross, and an Englishman made a rude one of a broken stick. She kissed it and laid it on her breast. The cross from a neighboring church was now brought, and she begged of her confessor, "Hold the cross up before me, that I may never cease to look upon it." As the crowd turned away from the market-place, one of the English leaders said fearfully, "We are all lost; we have burned a saint."

Jeanne's ashes were cast into the Seine; but her death aroused and united the French as even her life could not do. They fell upon the English with new energy, and before many years had passed, England lost every foot of French soil that she had once held, except Calais.

CHAPTER XV

PIERRE BAYARD, THE PERFECT KNIGHT

PIERRE BAYARD was born in a castle perched on a rocky crag in the mountains of Dauphiné, in France. It had dungeons and trap doors and gloomy passages, quite according to the old story books; but it also had a great hall with a cheerful wood fire, with rushes on the floor, and skins of bears and wolves laid here and there.

The four children, all boys, learned nothing of books, but they did learn to tell the truth, to say their prayers, and to fear nothing. They had a wild, happy, out-of-door life; but children grow up fast, and one day their father called them to him and asked what they would like to do when they were men. When it was Pierre's turn to choose, he said he wanted to be a knight, like his grandfather. "My boy," said his father, "you shall have your wish. Your grandfather was one of the best knights of his day, and I believe that you will not be unworthy of him."

The first step toward knighthood was to become a member of some household whose master was of high rank, and very soon the boy of thirteen was on his horse, ready to gallop away to become a page at the castle of the Duke of Savoy. When he said good-bye to his mother, she said, "My boy, I bid you to serve God and pray to Him morning and night; to be gentle and courteous to all; and to be charitable to the poor." Pierre promised her, and this promise he kept to the last day of his life.

In the castle of the Duke of Savoy Pierre learned to use arms, to run, leap, and swim, to play all sorts of athletic games, and never to fail in courtesy or in neatness of dress. He learned also to read and write, to play chess and backgammon and other indoor games. Before many months had passed, the duke decided to go to court and to take the young page with him. The king, Charles VIII, took a great fancy to Pierre and his wonderful riding, and in a fit of generosity the duke presented him with the boy. In the royal court he was taught still more of wrestling, fencing, of the use of the sword and the crossbow; and he learned so rapidly that when he was only seventeen he was made a squire.

Every man of arms longed, of course, to get a taste of real warfare; and Pierre was delighted when King Charles brought forward his claim to the throne of Naples and set out on an expedition to Italy. This did not accomplish much, but Charles's successor, Louis XII, was fully as eager as Charles to make conquests in Italy. The Pope, the Emperor of Germany, the King of Spain, and the King of England were all afraid of letting France become too powerful. They all fought against her, and it would seem as if even Bayard might have had enough of fighting; but he was never tired of it. Once when there was a truce of two months, he and a friend met a company of thirteen Spaniards and saluted them courteously. After a little conversation, one of the Spaniards said: "We are utterly tired of this truce, and perhaps you feel the same. Here are thirteen of us; supposing you and eleven others come out against us and see which side will conquer." Bayard was ready, of course, and a week later the fight took place.

This contest was somewhat like a tournament; that is, at a given signal the two parties put spurs to their horses, and with leveled lances galloped together to try to unhorse their adversaries. Now the armor worn in those days was very heavy, sometimes weighing as much as two hundred pounds, and the bravest knight in the field was helpless if once thrown from his horse. For this reason it was entirely against the laws of chivalry to aim at the horse of an adversary. The Spaniards, however, had a grudge against Bayard, and they paid no attention to this law, but aimed at the horses, and soon eleven of them lay dead. There was one result of the trickery, however, which they had not counted upon, for their own steeds refused to step over the bodies, and therefore the line of dead horses made so good a rampart that the two French knights, Bayard and his friend, rode away with the honors of the fight.

The story of this engagement was told and retold with the greatest delight by the admirers of Bayard; but perhaps they took even more pleasure in the tale of his holding the bridge quite in the fashion of Horatius of the early Roman days. When this took place, the French were encamped on one side of the river Garigliano in southern Italy, and the Spanish on the other side. The bridge was in the hands of the French, and Bayard, quite as a matter of course, had his quarters close to it; that is, in the place of greatest danger. One day the French were amazed to see that Spanish troops had succeeded in crossing the river by a ford and were coming up the bank. The whole army were upon them, the French thought. Bayard was always clear-headed, and he saw that there were not more than two hundred Spaniards, and that they were aiming at the bridge. He sent a messenger off at full speed for troops, and he took his stand at the end of the bridge, striking out so vigorously that, as the old chronicler says, the Spaniards thought they were fighting a devil and not a man. Reinforcements came to the French, and Bayard chased the Spanish over the bridge and a mile or two farther on the other side. Then seven or eight hundred men were seen coming to help them, and he ordered a retreat. He was last in line, and, when thirty or forty Spaniards surrounded him, he was forced to surrender. His friends turned and dashed upon the enemy to rescue him; but Bayard's captors had not realized what a prize they had taken, and they had not even disarmed him. His own horse was exhausted, so he sprang upon a fresh one belonging to the Spaniards and fought desperately. The end of it was that the Spaniards galloped away at full speed, while the French sat at ease on their horses, laughing to see them go.

The war continued, and now Venice joined the

Italian forces. The French king's nephew, Gaston de Foix, Duke of Nemours, was in command of the French. He was determined to capture the town of Brescia, strongly fortified as it was. All the knights agreed to his plan of attack except Bayard alone. "Our foot soldiers who are to lead the advance will have to meet picked men of the enemy," he said, "and I advise that they have one hundred and fifty horsemen to support them." "What you say is true," replied the duke, "but the first aim of the enemy would be to shoot every horseman. Who would put himself and his men at the mercy of the Italian arquebuses?" "I will," said Bayard quietly, "and I will answer for it that my company will do good service to our king." This was all the more noble in Bayard because he had such detestation of fighting with arquebuses or any other machines for throwing balls. To be slain in a contest of swords or lances or battle-axes he looked upon as fair and just, but, as he said, "It is a shame that a man of spirit should be exposed to be killed by a miserable stone or iron ball against which he cannot defend himself."

The attack upon the town began with such a noise of clarions and trumpets and drums that it was "enough to make the hair of the boldest stand on end," said one who was present. The troops in the town responded with volleys of cannon shot. These cannon cannot have been very dangerous, for it was said that one shot straight into the midst of the duke's company, but not a man was killed or wounded! Before long came the dash upon the walls.

Bayard was the first to cross the rampart, but he paid dearly for the honor, for he was wounded so severely that he had to be carried from the field. The French swore vengeance for the injury to their beloved knight and attacked the town more furiously than ever. Their valor was needed, for they had to meet not only the fire of the troops within the walls, but also the stones and bricks and boiling water and pieces of furniture which the women were throwing over the walls and down upon the besiegers. Nevertheless, Brescia fell.

On one occasion Bayard and his men were entirely surrounded in battle, and he was forced to advise them to yield. He caught sight of a Burgundian soldier too exhausted to think of taking prisoners. He had removed his helmet and sat on the bank of a stream. "Yield, or you are a dead man," cried Bayard, with his sword at the man's throat. "I yield," said the man, for he could do nothing else, "but who are you?" "I am the Captain Bayard," replied the knight; "take my sword, for now I yield myself to you." After a few days in camp, Bayard remarked that he wished to go home. "But we have said nothing about your ransom," exclaimed the Burgundian. "*My* ransom!" cried the knight. "But what about *yours?* I might have slain you if I had chosen. We'll fight it out between us." But the Burgundian had no wish to fight the great Bayard, and they agreed to leave the question to the commanders. So it was brought before the Emperor of Germany and the King of England, Henry VIII. The emperor looked at the king, and the king looked at the emperor. Finally they agreed — and Bayard and the Burgundian agreed with them — that the two prisoners might well consider themselves quits. Henry VIII afterwards offered Bayard great riches and honors to enter his service, but Bayard refused. "I have only one master in heaven, who is God," he said, "and one on earth, who is the King of France, and I shall never serve any other."

Bayard's death came about by the obstinacy of one Admiral Bonivet. In spite of Bayard's explanations that the place could not be held, the admiral insisted upon his occupying a little village with neither walls nor ditches nor barricades, and close to the camp of the enemy. Bayard did everything that a brave knight could do, but he was struck by a stone from an arquebus. "O God, I am slain!" he cried, and raising the cross-hilt of his sword to his lips, he kissed it as if it were a crucifix. His friends were about to carry him away, but he said: "I have never turned my back to a foe, and I will not do it now. Put me at the foot of a tree with my face to the enemy, and then charge upon them." After he had been laid tenderly down, he bade farewell and sent messages to his king and his friends.

When it was known that the great Bayard was dying, warfare was forgotten, and both friends and enemies gathered around him. Among them was the Constable of Bourbon, who had deserted the French king and entered the service of Spain. "How much I pity you," he said to the suffering knight; but

Bayard replied: "I thank you, but pity is not for me, who die a true man, serving my king. Pity is for you, who bear arms against your prince, your country, and your oath." The Italian Marquis of Pescara had his own tent brought for Bayard, and his own bed, and he himself helped to lay the wounded man upon it. In the midst of an earnest and trustful prayer to God to receive his spirit, the good knight passed away. He had been faithful to the three French kings under whom he had lived. He had fought with Italians, Spaniards, and Englishmen, and had won the respect of every adversary. He was the model of all chivalric virtues, a knight without fear and without reproach.

CHAPTER XVI

THE FIELD OF THE CLOTH OF GOLD

THE third of the three French kings who were served by Bayard was Francis I, who was somewhat of a spoiled child, but lovable and brave. One of his first exploits with the sword took place in a room of his own palace. He had just captured a wild boar in the forest, and for some whim let it loose in the courtyard. A little later, one of the doors was burst open, and in rushed the angry beast. The courtiers ran for their lives, but the prince drew his sword, and soon the dead body of the boar was tumbling down the stairs and back into the courtyard.

When Francis came to the throne, he was only twenty years old, and was longing for adventure and glory. The two preceding kings had gained nothing permanent in Italy, and Francis determined to do better. He crossed the Alps, building bridges and blowing up rocks to make a way for his army, and met the Italians, together with the Swiss, whom they had hired to help them, on the field of Marignano, and was victorious. "I have been in seventeen battles," said one of the French marshals, "and they have been only child's play compared with this."

Francis was not only brave himself, but he appreciated bravery in others, and before he left the battle-field he went straight to Bayard and said, "Bayard, I pray you to bestow upon me the honor of knighthood." "But, sire," replied Bayard, "the king of so noble a realm, he who has been crowned and consecrated with oil sent down from heaven, is knight over all other knights." "Bayard, my friend," returned the king, "make haste. Do not quote laws or canons here, but do my bidding." "Assuredly, sire," said Bayard, "I will do it, since it is your pleasure."

So it was that Francis was made a knight, and there on the field he knighted those of his followers who had done most valiant service. He gained no new dominions by his Italian wars, but he did gain new ideas of art and architecture, and when he returned to France, he carried with him paintings and statuary made by the greatest artists of Italy.

Francis delighted in magnificence and display, and only four or five years after the battle of Marignano, he had an opportunity to be just as gorgeous as he chose. A certain young Austrian prince by the name of Charles had by the death of one of his grandfathers become King of Spain, and also of Naples, Sicily, Sardinia, and the Netherlands. Then, too, this was in 1519, when Cortez was conquering Mexico, and great stores of gold and silver were coming into the coffers of Spain from the New World across the Atlantic. Charles was already a very powerful and wealthy monarch; and now, by the death of his other grandfather, Austria fell into his hands. Even worse than that, in the eyes of Francis I of France and Henry VIII of England, was the fact that he was soon chosen Emperor of Germany.

This put into his control all western Europe except France and the British Isles.

Francis and Henry had each hoped to be chosen emperor, and they were now two badly disappointed young monarchs. What could they do about it? Francis decided to make war against Charles, and Henry was apparently quite willing to unite with him. They agreed to meet and talk over their plans.

The place of meeting was to be near Calais, where English and French territory met, so that each king could be on his own soil. Splendid preparations were made by both sovereigns. Henry had sent eleven hundred skilled workmen from Holland and Flanders to build him a summer palace. Its windows were glazed with finer and more transparent glass than had ever been seen before. Posts and mullions were overlaid with gold. Statues of men in glittering armor were everywhere. Close to the entrance was a fountain flowing, not with water, but with wine, and over it in letters of gold was the inscription, "Make good cheer who will." Within the palace all things were rich and elegant. The ceilings of the corridors were covered with fluted white silk, and those of the chambers with roses on a golden groundwork. The hangings were of silk, of different colors and beautifully embroidered. Tapestry of silk and gold, Turkish cushions, cloths and draperies of golden tissue and rich embroidery adorned the state apartments.

Francis had put up a tent, but such a tent as never was seen before, for it was dome-shaped and covered with cloth of gold. It was lined with blue velvet studded with golden stars. Adjoining the tent were other tents, smaller, but just as richly decorated.

There were hundreds of tents for the members of the two courts, and banners of all colors floated above them. Coats of arms were emblazoned upon them, and at the door of each stood a sentinel with glittering bill and lance. Knights were all about in their dazzling armor. It is no wonder that from that day to this the plain has been known as the "Field of the Cloth of Gold."

But in the midst of all this splendor there was important business to attend to, and before long the two kings, most richly dressed, met and made a treaty which, among other provisions, bound the French king to marry the four-year-old daughter of the English king. The sovereigns made speeches of friendship, took wine together, and after the presentation of their respective courts, the meeting came to an end.

For more than two weeks there were feasts and tournaments and all kinds of entertainments. But through it all the officials of the two kingdoms feared treachery, and the two kings were obliged to meet with much formality. This was especially annoying to Francis, and one morning he slipped out of his bedroom and with only two gentlemen and a little page to attend him went to call on Henry. "Surrender, I have come to take the castle," he cried merrily to the astounded English guards. "Where is the chamber of the king, my brother?" he demanded. The governor of the palace did not dare refuse to answer, but pleaded, "Sire, the king is not yet awake." Francis went on, knocked at Henry's door and walked into the room. Naturally the English king was amazed, but also much gratified at the trust which the French king had shown in him. Henry gave his guest a jeweled necklace, and Francis presented to him in return a valuable bracelet which he had brought with him. "I will wait upon you," Francis declared, and, quite in the fashion of a valet, he handed King Henry his shirt and other clothes.

After this, everything was delightfully friendly between the kings and between their peoples; and yet, not long before Henry had crossed the English Channel, Charles of Spain had visited England, and Henry on his way home visited Charles in Flanders and spent three days with him in Calais, and when war broke out two years later he became the ally of the Spanish king!

Francis won no more such victories as that of Marignano, and at length, at the battle of Pavia, he was captured, and shut up in a gloomy Spanish prison. To win his freedom, he signed a treaty with Spain and delivered his two little sons to Charles as hostages. Before long he declared that since he had been forced to sign this treaty, it was not binding upon him, and war followed. He was ready to pay any price for the help of England, and Henry now joined the French side. This helped Francis very little, but in the peace that followed, the two boys were given back to their father. This time it was

Charles who broke the treaty, and war began again. So it went on till a short time before the death of the French king.

These wars, which lasted most of the time during a quarter of a century, aimed at preserving what is called the balance of power in Europe; that is, preventing any one country from becoming strong enough to control other countries. This struggle began in the reign of Francis, and has lasted for four hundred years, each nation living in fear lest some neighboring nation should become too powerful. It is this which has made it necessary to keep standing armies of troops always ready for warfare; and it is this which has increased so heavily the weight of taxation upon the people of European lands.

Francis was interested in the New World, and he sent out explorers in spite of the wrath and indignation of Spain and Portugal. These countries, because of their early voyages to America, claimed the whole continent; but Francis only laughed at their complaints, and returned the rather exasperating reply, "Show me the clause in the will of Father Adam which divides America between Spain and Portugal, and excludes France."

Francis appreciated art and architecture and music and literature. He built handsome palaces. He invited poets and artists and musicians to his court, and some of them made it their home. In such ways as these he did a great deal for his country, and if his life could only have been free from war, he would have been able to do much more.

CHAPTER XVII

THE STORY OF COLIGNY

IN 1522 the Marshal de Chatillon died, and his four little boys were left for their mother to bring up in the fashion thought proper for the children of a French nobleman.

Not so very many years earlier, boys in their position in life would have been taught to use arms, to be brave and fearless and courteous, and not so very much besides. If a letter was to be written, a clerk would write it. If a document was to be signed, a knight would make his mark and not feel in the least ashamed of being unable to write his name. But now times had changed, and it was looked upon as a disgrace for a young man of good family to know nothing of books. Of course, then, these boys had a tutor as well as an instructor in arms; and when they were brought to court, they were well fitted to take their place among the best-trained of the young nobles.

The dauphin, who afterwards became Henry II, was of about their age. He and Gaspard Coligny de Chatillon and the young men who gathered around the court, had the merriest time possible with tournaments, dances, tennis, hunting, and all the light-hearted pranks that a group of happy young men could think of. Often people like those best who are least like themselves, and the Duke of Guise, a young noble whom Coligny especially admired, was quite his opposite. Coligny was rather inclined to be grave and thoughtful. People had to know him well before they really appreciated him. The Duke of Guise was open-hearted in manner, merry, generous, and winning; and everybody, from King Francis to the boys in the streets, was devoted to him. King Francis, however, although he admired him, did not really trust him, and when about to die, he warned his son Henry not to allow the Guise family to become too powerful.

It was almost a matter of course that young men of good family should become soldiers. Coligny and Guise fought side by side in many a battle, and both soon won high promotion. Coligny was made captain-general of the French infantry, composed chiefly of Swiss, who could always be hired to fight for any one, anywhere. They were wild and lawless. They murdered and pillaged wherever they went. No one had ever tried to make them show any decency or honor. Imagine their wrathful surprise when Coligny ordered them to stop quarreling and swearing and pillaging and behave like respectable men. His penalties were not agreeable. If a man insulted a woman, he was to be hanged. If he made no effort to give up swearing, he was invited to spend eight days in prison on bread and water for his first offense. For his third offense, he lost one hand. Of course Coligny was called severe, but by the punishment of a few he saved thousands of lives and transformed a mob of robbers and murderers into well-behaved troops. Another reform of his, which probably the soldiers appreciated quite as much as being made to behave themselves, was the formation of an ambulance corps to carry the wounded to a military hospital, the first time that such a thing had ever been done.

Both Guise and Coligny were ambitious, of course, like any other young men of spirit, and both attained to high positions, for Guise became lieutenant general, and Coligny admiral.

In 1552, the king made war upon Charles V of Spain. Early in this war, Guise held Metz against all the attacks of the Spanish. He also took Calais, which had been in the hands of the English for more than two hundred years. Moreover, to add to all this glory, his niece married Francis, eldest son of King Henry. Coligny had been equally brave and skillful in the war, but less fortunate. He had held Saint-Quentin till its walls fell, and by this had saved Paris; but he had been obliged to surrender at last and had been taken prisoner.

While in prison, Coligny had time to think of religious subjects, as thousands of other people were doing. The Bible had been translated. People were reading it and were talking of matters of religion, and instead of accepting whatever the Church taught, they were discussing and questioning and making up their minds for themselves, and many were becoming Protestants, or Huguenots, as they were called in France. To leave the Roman Catholic Church and become a Huguenot was looked upon by all Catholics not only as accepting a wrong and dangerous belief, but also as taking a long step toward disloyalty to the king, which deserved heavy penalties. On the other hand, there were disagreements even among the Protestants, and they sometimes persecuted one another. Then, too, political interests entered into the matter. King Francis believed that to permit his subjects to become Protestants would weaken his authority; therefore he persecuted the French Huguenots. But to weaken the authority of Charles V in Germany was just what he wanted; therefore he aided the German Protestants. Coligny had long been inclined to favor the Huguenots, and when he was released from prison, he came out openly as one of them and soon became their principal leader.

King Henry's death left the crown to his sickly young son, Francis II, who had married Mary, Queen of Scots, niece of Guise. The Duke of Guise was then a successful general, uncle of the queen, a man of great ability and winning manners. Few boys of sixteen would have stood out against his advice, and King Francis was not one of those few. The Duke of Guise and his family were practically the rulers of the country.

But in less than two years Francis died, and Mary, Queen of Scots, was obliged to leave her beloved France and return to Scotland. Charles, the ten-year-old brother of Francis, now became sovereign. The land was in such disorder that civil war was probable. In the midst of the confusion, Coligny planned a settlement in America where the Huguenots might be free to think and to worship as they believed right. One attempt was made at the entrance of Port Royal, South Carolina, another on the Saint John's River in Florida. The first failed for lack of food; the second was destroyed by the Spaniards and most of the colonists slain — "Not as French, but as heretics," the Spaniards declared.

Catherine de' Medici, mother of the boy king, was regent. She was a woman quite without principles of honor and uprightness, and with a single aim, namely, to increase her own power. To weaken the power of Guise she allowed many privileges to the Huguenots. Then, when the Huguenots showed signs of becoming too strong to suit her wishes, she made a secret treaty with Charles V to destroy them and plotted with the Guise party to murder the Huguenot leaders. An attempt was made to kill Coligny; but King Charles was fond of Coligny and went at once to tell him how sorry he was. This alarmed Catherine. Evidently, if she was to retain her power, she must get rid of the Huguenots; so she and her followers planned a general massacre of them. She wrote a decree authorizing such a massacre and carried it to Charles to sign. He was now twenty-two years old, but he was almost as much under his mother's influence as when he was a boy. At first he refused. "But do you not realize," demanded Catherine, "that the Huguenots will all accuse you of encouraging the attack upon Coligny? They will rise up against you. Better to get rid of them now than to risk a battle later." Over and over Charles refused to sign the decree. Even after his mother succeeded in making him believe that the Huguenots were plotting against his life, he refused. Day after day she kept up her arguing and pleading. Then she began to weep and declared that she should leave the court. Charles had held out remarkably well for so weak a nature, but now he suddenly yielded. "Kill them all, then!" he cried. "Kill every Huguenot in France, so that none may be left to reproach me."

At two o'clock on the morning of Saint Bartholomew's Day, the ringing of a church bell was heard in Paris. Others followed, until there was a wild jangling from every belfry. This was the signal, and in a moment the streets were filled with armed men bearing on hat or sleeve a white cross, the badge of the Guise family. Every Huguenot, man, woman, or little child, that could be found was murdered.

Coligny was one of the first to die, for his old boyhood friend, the Duke of Guise, went at once to the house of his rival and sent assassins up the stairs to his bedroom. "Are you Coligny?" they questioned. "Yes, I am," Coligny replied calmly. "I am a wounded and aged man, and you ought to respect my gray hairs. But you will not shorten my life much," he added.

Catherine had also sent to the various provinces commands in the king's name to carry on similar massacres. Some of the governors obeyed; others refused. One wrote: "I respect Your Majesty too much not to believe that this letter is a forgery; and if, which God forbid, the order be genuine, I respect Your Majesty too much to obey you." Nevertheless, so many obeyed that it is believed twenty thousand Huguenots perished in France.

All Europe was horrified, all save Philip II of Spain, successor of Charles V. He sent a message to Charles that if soldiers were needed to complete the overthrow of the Huguenots, he should be glad to supply them. Catherine never expressed the least regret for the horrors of Saint Bartholomew's Day. Charles died after two years of keen remorse and physical suffering. And yet he had so little stability of mind that he appointed Catherine regent until his younger brother should be able to reign.

CHAPTER XVIII

KING HENRY OF NAVARRE

AT the death of Charles IX, there were three Henrys who were prominent in France. The first was Charles's younger brother, who now became Henry III.

Henry was already King of Poland, but he did not like Poland, and was so delighted to be able to return to France that he actually ran away from his kingdom. A crowd of his subjects ran after him, but they could not catch their fugitive sovereign. Henry amused himself in Italy for a while, and then went to France. The French people were ready to welcome their new king, but they soon found that there was nothing kingly about him except his title. He paid no attention to his royal duties, but idled his days away. Worse than this, he became the leader of a band of vicious, dissolute young men who filled their time with shameless acts.

It is small wonder that the French, both Catholics and Protestants, were indignant and disgusted. The Huguenots were becoming stronger, and the Catholics formed a League to uphold and protect their faith. Their leader was Henry, Duke of Guise, the second of the three Henrys.

The third Henry was Henry, King of Navarre, the leader of the Protestants. King Henry III of France had no children, and this Henry of Navarre, though only a tenth or eleventh cousin, was heir to the French throne.

King Henry III was about as foolish as a king could be. First, he gave privileges of worship to the Protestants, or Huguenots; which angered the Catholics. Then he took away these privileges; which angered the Protestants. The result was the "War of the Three Henrys," and before long there came a day which is known as the "Day of the Barricades," because the citizens of Paris made barricades of carts, barrels, and paving-stones, and stretched chains across the streets, in order to resist the king's troops. These troops had to yield, and King Henry, in his own capital, was forced to beg the Duke of Guise — whom he had forbidden to enter Paris — to try to stop the slaughter in the streets. The duke did this without the slightest trouble, for the Parisians were ready to obey his slightest wish. The king was forced to make the duke lieutenant-general of France and to agree to take up arms against the Huguenots.

Not many months later, the duke was called to the king's room. As he drew aside the portière, a group of assassins attacked him, and he fell dead at their feet. Henry kicked the body aside. "I am King of France now," he declared in delight; "the King of Paris is dead." Both Protestants and Catholics were horrified at the crime, and the Pope excommunicated King Henry. One day a young monk begged leave to present a letter to the king; and as Henry was reading it, the monk stabbed him to the heart. Thus ended the life of Henry III, the last of the House of Valois.

King Henry of Navarre was now King Henry IV of France. He was born in a castle in the Pyrenees, and was brought up by a wise mother and an equally wise grandfather. Nobody dreamed that he would ever become King of France, for nine princes stood before him in the succession to the throne. He was dressed like the other boys of the district, and scrambled up the mountains with them, barefooted and bareheaded. His food was the same as theirs — coarse bread, beef, cheese, and garlic; and they were not allowed to show him any deference because he was a prince. When he went to visit the French court, the court historian said of him that he was "the jolliest and best-composed lad in the world." His tutor was as sensible as his grandfather, and the boy was taught such rhymes as:

> "Kings rule their subjects with a mighty hand;
> But God with greater power doth kings command,"

and

> "Either justly gain the victory,
> Or learn with glory how to die."

When this "jolliest lad in the world" was fifteen, he was taken to the camp of the Huguenots and greeted as their leader. Before long he showed so much ability that he became their leader in reality as well as in name. It was fortunate that he had military talent, for after he became king, he had to spend five years fighting his way to Paris, the capital of his own kingdom. He won an important battle at Arques, and then came the battle of Ivry. It is of this that Macaulay wrote his poem, beginning,

"Now glory to the Lord of Hosts, from whom all glories are!
And glory to our sovereign liege, King Henry of Navarre!"

Just before the battle, King Henry rode along the lines with a snow-white plume in his helmet. "If my standard-bearers fall," he said, "press where you see my white plume shine, for there will be the thickest of the fight." The battle began and, as Macaulay tells the tale,

"A thousand spurs are striking deep, a thousand spears in rest,
A thousand knights are pressing close behind the snow-white crest;
And in they burst, and on they rushed, while, like a guiding star,
Amidst the thickest carnage blazed the helmet of Navarre."

Henry and his brave followers won the victory, and by and by he drew near to Paris. He besieged the city, but he never forgot that his opponents were also his subjects. More than once he permitted food to be carried within its walls, and he allowed thousands of non-combatants to withdraw. "I am their father and their king," he said. "They are innocent; it is the Leaguers that are resisting me." It is no wonder that the four thousand who were allowed to leave at one time marched out crying "Long live the king!"

Philip II of Spain sent troops to raise the siege; and before long Henry IV of France found himself in a difficult position. Any favor that he showed to either party aroused the other party against him. Even those to whom he had shown the favor felt no gratitude, for they always thought that he might have done more for them. The result was that hardly one sixth of the French were his friends. The League was against him. The Pope was against him. Queen Elizabeth of England was giving him some help, but not nearly enough. The French were planning to make the daughter of the powerful Philip II of Spain their queen. Just at this time Henry made up his mind to become a Roman Catholic. He went in state to the Abbey of Saint Denis, where he was met by the archbishop and many others of the clergy.

"Who are you?" demanded the archbishop.

"I am the King of France," Henry replied.

"What do you wish?"

"To be received into the bosom of the Catholic, Apostolic, and Roman Church," said Henry.

So it was that Henry IV became a Catholic. Whether he was convinced or not that his Protestant friends were "heretics," he had at any rate chosen the only way to keep the kingdom united and to save it from Spain, for within a few months he was accepted as king by nearly all France. He took no vengeance upon his enemies. When the Spanish troops left Paris, he saluted them and cried merrily, "Commend me to your master, gentlemen, but do not come here again."

Philip, however, did not give up the hope of setting the French crown upon his daughter's head, and for three years longer the war with Spain con-

HENRY IV AND MARIE DE' MEDICI

tinued. The royal treasury of France was emptied to pay the soldiers, and the king was poorer than his subjects. "My shirts are all torn," he wrote to a friend. "My doublets are out at elbows, my cupboard is often bare, and for the last two days I have been dining and supping with one and another." At length, however, Henry's enemies were overcome, and Philip II met his death.

Henry had become a Catholic, but he did not forget that many of his subjects were Protestants. In 1598 he issued a famous paper in their behalf, called the Edict of Nantes. This gave to both Catholics and Protestants equal rights in the practice of their religion and in holding office. It even established a special court to look out for their interests. To-day this would be regarded as no more than fair; but in those times it was looked upon as a wonderfully liberal proceeding.

Henry astonished the rulers of the other European countries in another way. It was generally accepted that a king had a perfect right to deceive others if he chose; but King Henry was so honest and sincere that they did not know what to make of him. It was a long time before they could believe that he really meant what he said.

King Henry had faults as well as people who are not kings; but he was one of the most unselfish of rulers. His first thought was always, "How can I help my people?" It is no wonder that his subjects loved him. "I want every peasant to have a fowl in his pot on Sundays," he said; and in those days, when peasants rarely tasted meat, this was a great wish. "Their father has come home," he said; and he set to work to study the wages and expenses of the working-people and to learn how much these wages would purchase for them. He lessened their taxes; he built roads and bridges; he drained marshes; he encouraged silk-making by planting mulberry trees to provide food for the silkworms; he built factories for weaving silk, velvet, lace, and linen, and for making glass. The country became happy and prosperous. Henry even sent out colonists to America, who founded Quebec. He planned a union of all the Christian nations of Europe against the Turks. But all this was suddenly brought to an end by the dagger of a half-crazed assassin. Paris was wild with grief. People ran about the streets groaning and weeping; and parents embraced their children, crying, "What will become of you? You have lost your father."

The French people have had rulers who were great, but no other sovereign has ever held such a place in their hearts as their beloved Henry IV.

CHAPTER XIX

THE RISE OF RICHELIEU

A FEW years before the death of Henry IV, a young man of a family called Richelieu was at a military school in training for the army. Suddenly he was called home by his mother and asked if he was willing to become a priest. In both army and Church there were opportunities to rise in the world; but in the Church there was a specially good opportunity for a son of the Richelieus. The family had been presented by King Henry III with the privilege of naming a bishop for the diocese of Luçon, and they wished to name this young Armand de Richelieu. The income of Luçon was not very large, but a bishop of even so small a diocese would always receive honor and be treated as a man of rank. To what position he might rise would depend in great degree upon himself.

Armand accepted the invitation. He promptly dropped his military pursuits and devoted himself to the study of theology and philosophy; and before he was twenty-three years of age, he had become Bishop of Luçon. According to the custom of the times, no one would have found any fault with him if he had made his home in Paris, where he could be at court and on the lookout for chances of promotion; but he went to the dirty little town of Luçon, to what he called the "most disagreeable bishopric in France," and did his best for his people.

The bishop was a poor man, but he was also a very ambitious man; and he never failed to have his eyes open to any opportunity to rise in the world. An opportunity soon appeared. When he had been at Luçon only three years, the murder of Henry IV took place, and a nine-year-old prince became Louis XIII and the ruler of France. His mother, Marie de' Medici, was made regent. "Woe to thee, O land, when thy king is a child," said a writer of the olden time; and the truth of this was soon evident in France. Confusion and discontent prevailed. The boy king was eager to rule, but he was allowed to have no power whatever. The queen was a weak, vain woman, who was controlled by an Italian and his wife. The nobles gathered around her. They cajoled and flattered her and begged for money and positions — which she gave to them for the sake of peace. Whether they were fitted for the positions into which she placed them was of no consequence to her or to them. She actually gave command of the whole French army to her pet Italian, although he had never been even a private soldier.

Such a condition of things could not last forever. Before long the money which Henry IV had left in the royal treasury had been handed out to the greedy nobles. They wanted more, and they felt sure that if they made life sufficiently unpleasant for the queen, she would manage in some way to get it for them. When she did not, they took up arms against her. Now was the time for the country bishop. He had made it plain that he was on the queen's side, and when she called a meeting of the States-General, he succeeded in being elected as a delegate of the clergy, and he made a speech or two that attracted attention. The wheels were beginning to turn.

All this time the boy Louis was becoming more and more indignant at being deprived of his birthright. When he was thirteen, he was declared of age; but the queen and her favorites showed no intention of allowing the rightful sovereign of France to share their power. Louis grumbled angrily, but he had not spirit enough to seize his proper position. Three years more passed, and then De Luynes, a man who took care of his hawks and who was a favorite of the king, persuaded him that the Italian was plotting to kill him. Louis was aroused. "You have my permission to arrest the man," he said, "and if he resists, to shoot him." Of course he resisted. Louis was watching, and when he heard the shot, he called out of the window to the murderers, "Thank you, thank you, I am king now." He really thought that if he was freed from the sway of his mother and her favorites, he would be able to rule; but De Luynes and the nobles were still much stronger than he. They now banished the queen; but the boy of sixteen soon found that he had no more power than before.

But what of the Bishop of Luçon in these years of confusion and snatching at money and offices? When the queen was sent away from court, he left court also, and followed her to her new abode, where she set up a court of her own. The bishop was now skillful enough to win the favor of both queen and king. He became chief of the queen's council — but refused to accept the office without the king's consent. He sent to De Luynes careful reports of whatever the queen might do — "to show that there is no reason for suspecting her," he assured one party; "to guard the king from any possible plots against him," he assured the other. He tried to make his faithfulness to the king very clear; but somehow neither Louis nor De Luynes was quite sure of it; and it may be that a hint from the king was what induced him to return to his diocese. After a while the queen became so troublesome that to prevent further difficulty the king was glad to have Richelieu return and act as her adviser.

Meanwhile, the Huguenots had risen against the royal forces. They planned to form a Protestant republic in the west of France with La Rochelle as its capital; and of course war resulted between the king and his Huguenot subjects. De Luynes, as the head of the army, was in command; and a strange commander he made, for he knew as little as a man could know about military matters, and even the private soldiers laughed at him. If he had been a very brave man, they would have respected him in spite of his ignorance; but they suspected that he was rather inclined to keep out of the way of danger.

De Luynes died of fever while the campaign was going on. What he would have done if he had lived is a question, for the Huguenots were in arms, the nobles were turbulent and rebellious, and Austria was becoming much stronger than was for the advantage of France. Now was the time for Richelieu. He had brought about peace between the king and his mother and, chiefly through the influence of Marie de' Medici, he was made a cardinal by the Pope. He soon became minister of state, and the most powerful man in France.

There was need of such a man. The king was keen enough to see it, and although he never really liked Richelieu, he kept him in office because this was for the interest of the country; and he followed the advice of his prime minister because it was the only thing to do. Cardinal Richelieu was the keenest politician France has ever known, and for a score of years he ruled king, council, and country. He was honestly devoted to France. He aimed at making her stronger than other European lands, especially Austria and Spain. One step toward this was to make an alliance with England. In France there was a princess of fourteen years, and in England there was a young prince in search of a wife. Richelieu brought it about that the two should marry. The princess was a Catholic, and he hoped that this marriage would make easier the lives of the Catholics in England. He was glad to do something for them, of course, but he was equally glad to form an alliance with the Protestant Dutch and Germans, because they were enemies of Austria. But while he was perfectly willing to marry the French princess to a Protestant Englishman and to join hands with Protestant countries if this would help to make France greater, he had no idea of permitting the Huguenots to become strong enough to have any political power in France. There was already warfare between them and the French Catholics. Before long it was plain that the party which could hold La Rochelle would be the winner. The Huguenots had fortified the city and were in possession. Richelieu besieged it. He had never forgotten his military training, and he commanded the siege in person. Even after twenty years as a bishop, he was still a soldier, and some one has pictured him in full military dress, with two pistols and a sword, and from his hat a long white plume floating as he allowed his horse to prance and caracole.

To capture this city was not an easy task. Troops could be stationed on three sides, and so prevent the sending of food by land; but there was the harbor, and it was a hard matter to keep ships from entering it, especially as King Louis had very few ships of war, and none at all that the defenders of La Rochelle could not easily overcome. In earlier struggles, Richelieu had borrowed vessels of Holland and England; but the Dutch did not care to assist the Catholics against the Protestants; and as for the English, they had before this declared that the French had not kept the promises of the marriage treaty, and instead of helping Louis, they did all that they could to help the Huguenots. They sent ships with food, and the French could not drive them away. At length Richelieu built of stonework directly across the mouth of the harbor a dike or mole almost a mile long; and this served his purpose well, for now the people of La Rochelle must either surrender or starve. They chose to starve. They lived on the flesh of horses, dogs, and rats; they boiled every scrap of leather that could be found and made a nauseous soup of this and any bit of green that they could discover. They held out for fifteen months, but finally they submitted; that is, the few who still lived submitted.

When the Huguenots had finally yielded, every one waited eagerly to see how the king — or rather, his minister — would treat them. A few were punished as rebels, but nearly all were pardoned. The Edict of Nantes was confirmed; the Huguenots were as free as the Catholics to practice their own form of worship. They were protected and treated with justice and considerable favor. Here the cardinal-general showed himself a shrewd politician. These Huguenots were industrious, thrifty people. Now that they were left free in matters of faith, they had no grievance against the king, and they became loyal subjects.

Richelieu's third aim was to lessen the power of Marie de' Medici and of the nobles. The queen-mother was indignant because Richelieu did not pay heed to her wishes, and she persuaded Louis to send the cardinal away from court. Fortunately, it was made clear to the king that this would be a great mistake. He and Richelieu had a talk together, and Richelieu unpacked his goods. The cardinal now punished severely those who had plotted against him, and the queen-mother left court.

This was a heavy blow to the power of the nobles; but they were even more alarmed and astonished to discover that in the rule of the cardinal all men were to be equal before the law. For instance, fighting duels was terribly common. A careless word or look might lead to a fight for life. There was a law against dueling, but no one paid any attention to it. Richelieu made a new law against the practice; but the number of duels became no smaller. Suddenly the nobles were amazed and aghast to find that the survivor of a duel, a member of a wealthy and powerful family, together with the seconds in the affair, had been executed as murderers. It was quite in style to be reckless of one's life; but to be put to death by the common executioner was another matter. It is no wonder that dueling went out of fashion.

The nobles were furiously angry, of course, but they were helpless, and they soon learned that under Richelieu's sway a man who broke a law was reasonably sure of punishment, and that it would not make the least difference whether he was a noble or a peasant. Another shock to the notions of the nobles was the lessening of the number of their fortresses; and still another was the appointment of officers to watch over the various provinces and so make sure that the nobles in power were governing them according to the laws of the land.

Richelieu died when only fifty-seven years of age,

saying, almost as his last words, "I heartily pray that I may be condemned if I have ever had other intentions than the welfare of the religion and of the state." In the eighteen years during which he was the real ruler of France he was always a friend to art and literature; he made his country the most powerful state in Europe; and he increased the royal power until the sovereign of France was almost unlimited in his supremacy. Whether this was for the good of the country and its people was left to later reigns to make manifest.

CHAPTER XX

LOUIS XIV AND VERSAILLES

NEARLY three hundred years ago, a little boy not yet five years old, with a mass of golden curls, sat in a great armchair and made a speech to the French Parliament. He said, "I have come to show my good-will. My chancellor will say the rest." This was Louis XIV, son of Louis XIII.

Of course there had to be a regency until the little king should be of age. His mother, the queen, was appointed. She chose as her chief adviser an Italian named Mazarin. He had worked under Richelieu, and Richelieu had recommended him to become his successor.

The small sovereign had come to the throne in the midst of the "Thirty Years' War." This had begun in a struggle between the Catholics and Protestants in Germany; but one country after another was dragged into it; and as the years passed, people actually forgot what the war was really about, but kept on fighting for power and territory. Fortunately for France, she had a brilliant general, the Prince of Condé, and a second almost equally brilliant, Turenne; and when the war finally came to an end, in 1646, her territory stretched out on the east to the river Rhine.

In spite of his great ability, Cardinal Mazarin was at first a very unpopular man, because he laid such heavy taxes on the people. The one that aroused them most was laid on all food brought into Paris by land or water. The Parisians were indignant, and the Parliament of Paris declared that this should not be permitted. In a day the streets of the city were filled with angry mobs, and probably King Louis himself heard them crying, "Down with Mazarin! Hurrah for our king!" Parliament told the queen how dangerous this uprising of the people might become. "If harm is done, you shall answer for it," she retorted in a rage, and rushed back to her room, slamming the door behind her. She and Mazarin took the little king, now ten years of age, and went away from Paris to a half-furnished palace a few miles away.

These street contests were the beginning of what is called the "War of the Fronde." At first the Parliament and the people of Paris were on one side, and the queen and her friends on the other; but before long, it turned into a wild tangle. There was a good deal of fighting, and there was a good deal of calling one another hard names and making absurd cartoons of one side and the other. The very name by which the war is called is a jest, for "fronde" was the name of a little sling which boys played with in the streets. All Paris sang,

> "A Fronde-ly wind
> Got up to-day;
> 'Gainst Mazarin
> It howls, they say."

For the greater part of five years this absurd imitation of war continued. It was often mere amusement for the nobles; but for the peasants, whose harvests were trampled down, cattle stolen, and homes burned, it was anything but amusement.

Meanwhile a real war between France and Spain was going on; and this did not come to an end until the Peace of the Pyrenees, in 1659. Both countries were tired of war, but to persuade them to agree on terms of peace was not an easy thing to do, and even the enemies of the cardinal recognized his rare tact and ability.

Mazarin, however, was planning more than the peace. Louis was sixteen years old, and it was high time for him to be married, thought Mazarin, but who should be his bride? Louis himself was much pleased with Mazarin's niece, but the wise cardinal knew that such a marriage would not be suitable for the King of France, and the maiden was sent to a convent. There was a certain princess of Savoy who had been proposed for Louis's queen, but the cardinal had not worked in vain, and one evening late in 1659 he entered the queen's room joyfully. "Good news, Madame," he cried. "Is it to be peace?" the queen asked. "More than that," replied the cardinal. "I bring you peace and the infanta." A paper was given to the disappointed princess of Savoy, promising her the hand of the king, provided the Spanish marriage did not take place within a year.

It did take place, however. Maria Theresa, the

Spanish princess, promised that neither for herself nor any child that she might have would she make any claim to the throne of Spain. Spain agreed to pay a large dowry, and all went on merrily.

The cardinal was at the height of his glory. He had brought about peace, and he had joined in marriage the royal families of Spain and France. But his health was failing rapidly, and within two years after the Peace of the Pyrenees he died.

Louis was eighteen. He had been declared of age five years before, but he had made no attempt to lessen the cardinal's authority. "I put up with it," he had said long before, "because of the good service he has rendered me; but I shall be master in my turn." Mazarin's last word of advice to the king had been, "Manage your affairs yourself, sir," and Louis followed the advice. The first official who came to him after Mazarin's death and asked to whom he should go for orders was met by the king with a decided "To me."

Louis did not intend to rule ignorantly, and he set to work to understand the business of being King of France. For eight hours a day he gave close attention to public matters. The courtiers smiled behind his back. "That won't last long," they whispered, but it did last. He had faults enough for two kings, but all through his long reign he was an industrious, persevering worker. If this work had been to help the French people, he could have done a great deal for them; but unfortunately Louis's one care was to win glory for himself. It was his business to command, and the business of every one else to obey, this monarch firmly believed.

Louis was keen to see who could serve him well, and for minister of finance he chose an honest man named Colbert, who had worked his way up in the world by his own merits. Colbert's chief business was to provide money for the king by taxation. In France at that time the rich nobles and clergy paid almost no taxes, while the poor were taxed to the last penny. Colbert could not change all this in a moment, but he did much to make life easier for the poor, for, just as far as possible he had taxes laid on houses, lands, income, and luxuries. He introduced some of the most famous manufactures of France, such as the making of china, tapestry, lace, and rich materials for dresses. This not only increased the revenues, but it gave employment to thousands of people, and thus France became prosperous. He improved the roads, and they were sadly in need of improvement. He made canals, and he built ships, both ships of war and merchantmen. Colbert was working for the good of France and its people, but Louis was working for himself and his own glory and amusement.

In spite of Colbert's excellent management, it was sometimes all that he could do to provide money for the king's demands. Louis spent a vast amount in war, for to him victorious warfare was the greatest glory on earth. He began with a war against the Spanish Netherlands on the ground that as Spain had never paid Maria Theresa's dowry, she was not bound by her promise to claim no Spanish possessions. The two great generals, Condé and Turenne, planned the campaigns, assisted by the military engineer Vauban, and Louis was successful. More territory was added to France, and the country became the most powerful in Europe.

Warfare was not the only way in which Louis was extravagant by any means. He loved magnificence, and he determined to build a palace that should be worthy of even so great a monarch as he thought himself to be. This palace was the famous Versailles, in which the makers of the Peace Treaty and the League of Nations met in 1919.

The best architects were employed to plan this palace. The best artists decorated its walls. Tapestries, paintings, and carvings were everywhere. Orange trees grew in silver tubs; silver candlesticks, chandeliers, railings, and benches were to be seen, and a silver throne eight feet high. Everywhere were statues and paintings of Louis in different costumes. Mirrors reflected the magnificence of the endless number of apartments.

Around this palace was an immense park, sixty miles or more in circumference. Here were groves formed of large trees brought from a distance. Here were lakes and fountains almost without number. At first, force pumps supplied them with water from the Seine River; but later a stream ninety miles away was turned from its course and brought into the grounds. Colbert lectured the king in most daring fashion on his extravagance. He said bluntly,

"It has seemed to me that you were beginning to prefer your pleasures and your diversions to everything else." But the king paid no heed to his wise minister.

Louis gathered to his court the most talented men of his time. Here were not only the greatest nobles and public men, but also the most illustrious poets, scholars, and artists of France. It was a glorious society, but Louis's chief enjoyment of it was in obliging all these men of talent to pay him reverence. He taught them that it was an honor to serve him in any way, even to hand him his shirt when he dressed in the morning.

Life at Versailles was as extravagant as the palace itself. It was always gorgeous, but at any fête the costumes were most magnificent. Cloth of silver embroidered with silver, cloth of gold sprinkled with diamonds, black velvet with great diamonds for buttons, head-dresses covered with jewels — it reads like a tale from fairyland. Even the every-day life of the king was full of ceremony, which he heartily enjoyed. Ordinary dressing was with him a lengthy proceeding, for each article had to pass through the hands of at least two persons. It actually required two pages to carry away his slippers. A special official presented him with his handkerchief, and another official gave him his stockings.

But this *lever*, or arising, of the king was not in point of ceremony to be compared with his public dinners. Merely spreading the table was a matter of much form and state. To bring in the food required a long procession. Guards, ushers, the "Gentleman Servant of the Pantry," the "Equerry of the Kitchen," the "Chief of the Goblet," the "Chief of the Wine Cellars," and a great number of other officials formed in line and solemnly marched up staircases, along several corridors, through vestibules and salons and ante-chambers, to the king's apartments. It was all very imposing, but the food must have been a bit cold before it reached His Majesty; and even after it had come, every dish had to be tasted before the king touched it, lest it should contain poison. There was just as much formality in eating as in bringing in the food. If the king wanted a sip of wine, the cup-bearer cried in a loud voice, "The drink for the king!" and it took the services of four more people before the wine could reach the royal lips. During the dinner, all well-dressed persons were allowed to file through the room; and people went to watch the king eat just as they go now to the circus or the zoölogical gardens to watch the animals fed.

For forty years King Louis had pretty much his own way. His courtiers looked upon him as almost a god — or made him think that they did. His wars were successful. France had become larger and more prosperous, and he had in general much more money than was good for him. Then came a change. Maria Theresa died, and the following year he married Madame de Maintenon, a lady of good family but no fortune. She was his wife, but she was never recognized as queen. She had been educated as a

Protestant, but had become a Roman Catholic; and she did much to persuade Louis that he ought to permit no Protestantism in his kingdom. He first tried to persuade the Huguenots to change their faith. Then he commanded all women not of noble birth who were found at their religious meetings to be whipped and branded. He quartered soldiers in the homes of the Huguenots with orders to torment them as much as possible. At length he revoked the Edict of Nantes. The Huguenots were forbidden to leave the country, but two or three hundred thousand contrived to escape. Most of these were skilled workmen, and other countries were delighted to receive them. So it was that Louis made his own country poorer, while Holland, England, and Germany became richer through the labor of these industrious people.

In 1688, several of the countries which Louis had injured united against him, and after a war of eight years he had to restore nearly all that he had taken in his earlier attacks. The throne of Spain had become vacant, and Louis placed his grandson upon it. Then Europe was indeed aroused, for if France and Spain were united under one ruler, no other country could stand against them. The Grand Alliance was now formed, a union of Louis's opponents, and warfare went on for twelve years. At its close, Louis's grandson, Philip V, was allowed to keep the crown of Spain, but Louis had to give back the Netherlands to Austria, and to give up to England the French colonies in Nova Scotia.

Two years after the close of this war, Louis died. He left his kingdom deeply in debt, few of its people living in comfort, and many of its people beggars. Commerce was ruined. Wide stretches of the country were left barren. The time of Louis is spoken of as the greatest age of France, but that is because so many famous men lived in his day — writers, artists, generals, admirals, and ministers of state. The heir to the kingdom was Louis's greatgrandson, a little boy of five years. The dying king realized some of his faults, and he said to the little child: "I have loved war too much. Do not be like me in that, nor in the useless spending of money. Try to improve the condition of your people."

CHAPTER XXI

THE FRENCH REVOLUTION

If Louis XV, successor of Louis XIV, had been a strong, upright man, a vast amount of trouble might have been prevented. But with a helpless little child for king, and powerful, vicious men for regent and prime minister, poor France had a hard time.

As the years passed, matters grew worse and worse, abroad as well as at home. In the "Seven Years' War," Quebec was captured by the English general Wolfe, and thus France lost Canada. The French power in the East was destroyed, and India fell into the hands of the English. The French Government became so weak and uncertain that the citizens despised it. They hoped that when the king should die, a change of rulers would better things; but he lived on year after year, nearly sixty years of misery for his people.

France in the eighteenth century was not a good country to live in. Taxes were terribly high, and there were three which the peasants found almost unendurable. One of these was the heavy tax on salt, especially unfair because each family was forced to buy of the Government a certain quantity, whether it was needed or not. One required them to labor on the roads and other public works whenever they were called upon, even though their crops might be spoiling in the fields. A third tax was levied according to the amount that a man's land produced. If a peasant adopted wise means of agriculture and raised good crops, his taxes increased. If two men, one industrious and one lazy, had the same kind of land, the man who worked hard and raised a large crop had to pay higher taxes than the lazy man.

This was bad enough, but it would not have been quite so hard to bear if all the people had been treated alike. On the contrary, the nobles paid hardly any taxes, neither did the bishops and archbishops nor the wealthy monasteries. The peasants and the country clergy, who were in general poor and needy, were almost the only ones to be taxed. The nobles despised the peasants, and the peasants hated the nobles. Meanwhile, a group of writers had much to say about freedom and justice and the rights of men, and tried to make the French understand how wrong and unfair all this was. People began to think.

When Louis XVI, grandson of Louis XV, came to the throne, he was only twenty years old. He had never expected to become king and, like other young nobles, he had spent most of his time amusing himself. His amusements were innocent enough, for he read substantial books; he liked geography and mathematics, and he especially enjoyed outdoor exercises and making locks and keys at a forge which he had set up in the palace. He had married when he was sixteen a young Austrian princess, Marie Antoinette. She was bright and pretty and charming, and if she had tried, she could have made every one love her. Instead of this, she thought of nothing but amusing herself. The manners of the ladies of the court were much more formal than she had been used to in her Austrian home, and their dress struck her as comical and old-fashioned. When they appeared before her, she made fun of them almost to their faces. Their banquets were stiff and lengthy, and she would not be bored by attending them. She liked to go on merry little picnics with people who were amused by her witty speeches. She built a country house called Petit Trianon, and there she used to make butter like a farmer's wife and, dressed as a shepherdess, to drive a flock of well-washed sheep with blue ribbons around their necks. Her husband sometimes played the game with her, and, pretending to be a miller, ground grain into flour for her to use in her cooking.

This was harmless, to be sure, but the king and queen of France had important duties to the nation, and these they were neglecting for amusement. Then, too, many of Marie Antoinette's entertainments cost a great deal of money, so much that it was sometimes difficult for the minister of finance to pay the bills. Her mother, the Empress of Austria, wrote her anxious, motherly letters, warning her that trouble would surely result; but the young queen went on in her own willful way.

Louis was upright and kind-hearted and desirous of doing all that he could for his people, but he was weak, and thought one thing one day and quite the opposite another day. Moreover, he was very fond of his wife, and she had little trouble in leading him wherever she wished.

Before long there were stories that the queen was using the money of the state for her extravagant entertainments. The French hated Austria, and they began to speak of the young queen as "the Austrian." Some even whispered that she was sending good French money to Austria. Mobs in the streets began to sing,

"My little queen, not twenty-one,
Maltreat the folk as you've begun,
And o'er the border you shall run."

Whatever might be the cause, the fact was certain that thousands of people in France were hungry, and even the royal treasury was empty. Louis had made a wise financier named Turgot minister of finance. He planned to reduce expenses and to tax all at the same rate. Then there was an outcry. The queen was indignant at the idea of reducing her expenditures; the nobles were angry at the thought of having to pay taxes; and even the peasants were annoyed at the changes which Turgot suggested, lest these should result in even worse than had yet come to them.

After a while the king gave up supporting Turgot, and a Swiss named Necker took his place. This was in the time of the American Revolution; and the money with which France helped the American colonies was another strain upon her resources. Necker was dismissed, and matters went from bad to worse. With an empty treasury and a hungry people, the queen and court were amusing themselves as usual. Louis was unhappy, but helpless.

Another minister of finance was tried, one De Calonne. His plan was to raise money by borrowing — but he made no provision to pay even the interest on this borrowed money. Necker was recalled, and he advised the king to call a meeting of the States-General; that is, representatives of the nobles, the clergy, and the "Third Estate," or commoners. The demand rang from one end of the land to the other, and the meeting was called. It was a brilliant assembly, for king and court came in their plumed hats and satin and velvet clothes embroidered with gold and jewels. The clergy wore flowing mantles, the archbishops in purple velvet, the others in colors varying according to their degrees. The Third Estate were ordered to wear short black cloaks and white cravats, and of course looked far inferior to the others in all their gorgeousness.

The Third Estate were not in brilliant attire, but they had done some thinking, especially on the question of how the voting should be done. There were more of the commons than of the nobles and higher clergy together; but it had been expected that each order would vote separately. In this case, the one vote of the Third Estate could do nothing against the two votes of the other divisions. The Third Estate, however, demanded that all should vote together. This would give them a majority, and naturally the nobles and higher clergy refused. The Third Estate thereupon named themselves and those of the other two orders who had joined them the National Assembly, took an oath not to dissolve till they had given France a constitution, and proceeded to business. At first Louis opposed, then he yielded; then, on his wife's advice, he called out some Swiss and German troops to protect him and keep order in Paris.

There was certainly need of some power to keep order. The mob seized bread, wine, and arms wherever they could be found. They put on cockades of red, white, and blue as badges, and for three days they raged up and down the streets of Paris. A report was spread, "The king is going to break up the National Assembly and turn the guns of the Bastille upon the city if there is any resistance." And at this all Paris went wild.

The Bastille had been built for a fortress, but from the time of Richelieu it had been used as a prison, and here men who had offended the king or some powerful noble had often been kept for years with no trial and sometimes with no charge brought against them. Whenever the French people looked at its massive walls, they thought of tyranny and injustice, and now they declared that they would have no more of it. They rushed roaring and howling through the streets, and after a five-hours' siege the Bastille was in their hands. The governor and his officers were murdered and their heads placed on pikes and carried about the city with wild shouts of rejoicing.

But where were the king and queen and nobles?

They were in beautiful Versailles, dancing and feasting and enjoying themselves. They knew that there was trouble in Paris, but they had no idea that it would affect them. After the king had gone to bed, a noble went to his room. "Sire," he said, "the Paris mob have taken the Bastille." "Why, that is a revolt!" said the king in bewilderment. "No, sire," declared the noble gravely, "it is a revolution."

Only a few weeks passed before the frenzy broke out again. Some new guards were sent to Versailles, and the old guards welcomed them with a banquet. When the king and queen entered the room, the soldiers cheered, tore off their red, white, and blue cockades and put on the white ones that were the royal emblem. It was not long before the story of this banquet reached Paris, and thousands of women caught up knives, brooms, pikes, sticks — whatever they could find — and rushed off to Versailles. "Take us to the king!" they cried. "Give us bread, bread!" Louis promised to send bread to them in Paris, but that was not enough; he must go with them, they declared. The National Guard, with the Marquis de Lafayette at its head, arrived and did its best to protect the royal family; but the mob was wild with excitement and hunger. Both Louis and the queen stepped out boldly on a balcony. "I am ready to die," said Marie Antoinette fearlessly. Lafayette knelt before her and kissed her hand. Even the rough crowd were touched, and she was saved.

But the mob were shouting, "The king to Paris!"

and Louis could not refuse. It was a strange procession — the king, queen, their two children, and the king's sister in a carriage, followed by a hundred deputies. Behind them swarmed thousands of the worst rabble in Paris, shouting, howling, screaming out coarse songs. A drizzling rain was falling. So it was that Louis and his queen were taken to the Tuileries. This palace had not been occupied for a long time. It was forlorn and gloomy, but here the royal family spent a year. The king hunted — though always in charge of some of the National Guards. The queen and Madame Elizabeth, the king's sister, sewed and taught the children and cared for them, the little six-year-old dauphin and his older sister Maria Theresa; and so the time passed slowly away in anxiety and dread of what might come.

The National Assembly had now prepared a constitution according to which the country should be governed. Lafayette, representing the National Guards, took the oath to observe it. He was followed by the National Assembly, and many other bodies of men; last of all by King Louis himself.

There was a great celebration, and all looked promising; but, nevertheless, the royal finances were in as bad a condition as ever, and there was no one who had the power and authority to make the people keep order. A strong king would have enforced the laws, and thus made his own position stronger and strengthened his country; but Louis was not a strong king. Mirabeau, who was the real head of the National Assembly, could have advised and helped him, but Marie Antoinette did not trust Mirabeau. Then, too, she had not yet given up the hope that by help of the other nations the old times might after a while be brought back again.

Mirabeau had shown himself sensible and reasonable. By his eloquence he had generally been able to bring the other members of the Assembly around to his own way of thinking, and thus had prevented much violence. As long as he lived, the king was safe; but he died the year after the acceptance of the Constitution, and now Louis felt that his life was in danger. Three members of the National Assembly, Robespierre, Danton, and Marat, were now in power. They belonged to what was called the Jacobin Club, because it met in an unused monastery dedicated to Saint James. There were many clubs in those times, and the Jacobin was the fiercest and most bitter of them all.

The king had good reason to fear, and he made up his mind to flee — or Marie Antoinette made it up for him. Many nobles who had before this fled from France had appealed to other kings to come to the aid of their sovereign. The interest of these rulers needed no arousing, for they had been anxiously watching the acts of the revolutionists lest trouble of the same sort should arise in their own domains. A general faithful to Louis was near the frontier with some troops. If Louis could come to him, a foreign army would be at hand to help him regain the power that had slipped from his hands.

Unluckily, the heads of the royal family knew about as much of the proper way to manage their flight as did the little dauphin. Every hour counted, but they made their preparations as leisurely as if they were going on a pleasure trip. Then, instead of trying to slip away from Paris in an ordinary carriage, they rode off in a large new coach of gorgeous yellow, with attendants in yellow livery and troops posted along the road. The harness broke more than once; the roads were muddy; the relay horses were not found where they were expected; and the fugitives spent twenty-two hours in going sixty-nine miles. Of course every one gazed at the big yellow coach; and before long they gazed straight into the face of the king, for he was so foolish as to show himself at the window. The result was that a very sober royal family were carried back to the Tuileries, and guards were placed about them, even in their bedrooms.

No one knew when foreign troops might invade France, and volunteers rushed to Paris. One company came from Marseilles, and as they marched into the city, they sang a thrilling song which, because of the place from which they came, was called the "Marseillaise." Its chorus is,

> "To arms, to arms, ye brave!
> The avenging sword unsheath!
> March on, march on, all hearts resolved
> On liberty or death!"

The Jacobins determined to attack the Tuileries, and the royal family fled to the Assembly for protection. The mad rabble fell upon the beautiful palace. They destroyed everything that could be destroyed, and killed every living creature within its walls. The king and his family were carried to prison, and every one who was believed to sympathize with them had the same fate. Danton was the leader of the furious mob. "When we go forth to defend our country," he declared, "the Royalists within the prison walls will break out, and neither mother, wife, sister, nor child will be safe from their revenge. Our only safety is to destroy them now." Then began a terrible massacre of the Royalists, not only in Paris, but all over France. Swords and pikes and guns did not do the work fast enough, and an instrument, known as the "guillotine" was used for beheading people.

King Louis was summoned before what was called the National Convention. He was quiet and self-controlled, and he answered all questions with good sense and dignity. He was accused of treason, of misgovernment, and of plotting against France with the enemies of the French people. Many of the members of the Convention would have defended him if they had dared; but Danton and the other Jacobins triumphed, and it was voted that within twenty-four hours he should die. The one favor granted him was to say good-bye to his family, from whom he had been separated for some time. A few hours later, he was taken to the guillotine. "Frenchmen," he said, "I die innocent. I pardon my enemies. I desire that France —" but the order was given to beat the drums. "Son of Saint Louis, ascend to heaven," said the priest who had heard his last confession, and the heavy knife of the guillotine fell.

During reign after reign the people had suffered because of the crimes and the mistakes of their rulers. This suffering had come to a climax in Louis's day, and it would have needed a far wiser man than he to rescue the land from the horrors of the Revolution which was upon it. Louis was kind and brave and meant to do his best, but he had not the wisdom to save his country or himself.

Among those who voted for the king's death were many who would, as has been said, gladly have done otherwise. These and others who were not so savage as the Jacobins were known as "Girondists," because the chief ones among them came from the Department of the Gironde. But the Jacobins were the stronger. They threw into prison all whom they suspected of disagreeing with them. When the prisons were full, the prisoners were turned out, hundreds at a time, old and young, rich and poor, innocent and guilty, and were guillotined. Even the guillotine did not work fast enough for the slaughter, and crowds of prisoners were made to stand between two great ditches. Cannon were fired at them, and as they fell into the ditches, earth was shoveled over their bodies, many still alive. It is said that fifteen thousand of the inhabitants of a single city which ventured to resist the rule of the Jacobins were put to death in these ways and in others still more terrible.

The Revolutionists abolished the Christian religion, and declared themselves worshipers of the Goddess of Reason. To show that the past was entirely gone by, they gave up Sunday and declared every tenth day a time of rest. The names of days and months were changed. The tombs of the kings in Saint Denis were broken open and the bodies thrown into quicklime. That of Henry IV, who had been so loved by his people, was set upright to serve as a target for all who wished to stone it. People were wild with a frantic rage for blood and destruction. Women used to go early to the places of execution in order to get good seats for watching the guillotine do its dreadful work. They carried their knitting with them, and marked off in their stitches the number of the slain. Such was the "Reign of Terror."

Marie Antoinette, her golden hair turned to gray by the horrors through which she had passed, was kept in prison. She was quiet and dignified and patient. She taught her children and did needlework, and so the dreadful days passed. Only a few months after the king's death, her children were taken from her. The dauphin, who had been so loved and so tenderly cared for, was given over to a cruel, brutal man. Then the queen was shut into a dark cell, her work taken away; and there she sat, waiting for the end. It came before many months had passed. She was condemned to die, and in a rough cart she was carried with fast-bound hands to the guillotine. She walked calmly and firmly up the steps of the scaffold. "Farewell, my children," she said. "I am going

MARIE ANTOINETTE IN THE CONCIERGERIE PRISON

to your father." The axe fell. "Long live the Republic!" shouted the crowd. The mad revolutionists of France had murdered their king and their queen. The little dauphin died from abuse and neglect. His sister lived, but her life was always saddened by the memory of those fearful days of suffering and terror.

The three men who had been leaders in these awful scenes met the fate that they deserved. A young girl named Charlotte Corday was convinced that if Marat was only dead, the horrors would cease. She pretended that she had important news for him, and he consented to see her. In a moment her dagger had done its work. But Robespierre, the most bloodthirsty of the three, still lived. In jealousy he had had Danton put to death, and now he stood alone. But the time came when his friends as well as his foes feared for their lives, and without regard to party they united, and Robespierre himself died by the guillotine.

The worst of the mad fury had come to an end, but there were different parties even in the National Convention, and whatever party was in power for the moment seized the opportunity to behead all opponents. At length, however, the country became more quiet. Many thousands still in prison were set free; and the members of the Convention went to work to make a republican constitution, for they had decided that France was henceforth to be a republic.

CHAPTER XXII

LAFAYETTE, FRIEND OF THE UNITED STATES

In the court of Louis XV was a bright, gentlemanly boy who served as a page. He also had the honor of being a commissioned officer in the bodyguard of the king, to which none but descendants of the most highly titled families were admitted. He was a marquis, he had a large fortune, and altogether he was looked upon as being a most lucky young man.

It was this same fortune, however, which stood in his way when it was proposed that he should marry a little twelve-year-old countess. "The Marquis de Lafayette has too much money," the mother of the girl objected. "He has neither parents nor near relatives, and he is free to spend it as he likes. That is not good for a boy." But after a while, when she came to know the boy better, she very willingly gave her consent. The young man of sixteen and the girl of fourteen were married and, as the old story books say, "lived happy forever after."

Two years later, 1776, was the year of the American Declaration of Independence. Lafayette was intensely interested in the struggles of the colonists, and he made up his mind to cross the ocean and put his sword at their service. His plans had to be kept secret, for Louis XVI, who was now on the throne, had not decided whether to help America or not. He would have liked the Americans to win, and so prevent England from holding the continent across the seas; but on the other hand, he did not wish to join them if they were going to lose and leave him entangled in a needless contest with England. Just then the Americans had met with so many defeats and misfortunes that it seemed as if they must lose the war.

It is no wonder that King Louis hesitated; but Lafayette did not. Mr. Silas Deane, representative in France of the colonies, had already, in the name of Congress, appointed him a major-general in the American army; and although he was told frankly how hopeless affairs now seemed and that the Americans could not even provide him with a passage to America, he merely thanked the commissioners courteously and said that he would purchase a vessel for himself. The king forbade his sailing, and this meant that disobedience might bring about the confiscation of his estates; but he sailed with eleven companions, and after a voyage of two months landed near Charleston, South Carolina.

As soon as possible, he presented Mr. Deane's letter to Congress, but Congress was in a difficult position. Mr. Deane had given many such letters, and it was not easy to determine whether a rich young fellow of nineteen, who had come across in his own vessel, was in earnest in wishing to lend a hand, or whether he was only an adventurer in pursuit of cheap glory. Congress made a very natural mistake and told the marquis that there was small prospect of an opening for him. A little man would have turned the prow of his ship away from the American shores, but this young Lafayette was not a little man. He dashed off a note to Congress which said: "After the sacrifices I have made, I have a right to exact two favors: One is, to serve at my own expense; the other is, to serve as a volunteer." Congress understood now with what sort of man it was dealing. His services were gratefully accepted, his appointment as major-general was confirmed, and before long he was attached to Washington's staff.

For four years and a half Lafayette worked eagerly for America. He gave his money lavishly; he fought brilliantly; he was wounded in our defense; he showed himself a wise strategist; and he was successful in that most difficult piece of generalship, the skillful management of a retreat. The British general Cornwallis declared that "the boy cannot escape me." But not many weeks later, "the boy" was publicly thanked by Washington for his distinguished service in the capture of the British general.

The friendship between Washington and Lafayette was most beautiful. "I love him as a son," said the commander to the surgeons who were to care for Lafayette's wound. To Lafayette himself the cool, reserved Washington wrote, "I love everybody that is dear to you." "In your friendship I find a delight which no words can express," Lafayette wrote to his American friend. Who can tell how much the affection of this devoted lover of liberty may have done to comfort and strengthen the greatest of Americans in his almost impossible task?

Lafayette's services to America were not limited to the field of battle. King Louis had at length yielded to the demands of his people, recognized the United States as an independent country, and sent a fleet to their help. Chiefly through the influence of Lafayette, who had returned on a short furlough, he was persuaded to send also a land force. Lafayette was received in France with the greatest honors, and he used his popularity to win favors for America. "It is fortunate," said the prime minister, "that Lafayette did not want to strip Versailles of its furniture for his dear Americans, for nobody would have been able to resist his earnestness."

In 1781, at the close of the American Revolution, Lafayette returned to France. Marie Antoinette and her friends were enjoying themselves. Necker's attempts to induce her to be less extravagant had aroused their wrath, and they were all rejoicing because Louis had put De Calonne into his place. De Calonne was the borrower who planned no means of payment, and when the treasury showed a deficit of millions of francs, his only suggestion was to hold a "Convocation of the Notables"; that is, men of rank or political prominence. Most of the members thought only of how to continue their idle, useless lives, but Lafayette reviewed the injustice and oppression of the peasants and showed how the court squandered the money of the people. "The millions which are thrown away are collected by taxation," he declared, "and taxation can only be justified by the real wants of the state" — rather a venturesome speech, considering that the king's brother was presiding at the Convocation.

When the National Association was formed, Lafayette did his best to persuade the nobles to unite with the commons, but in most cases he failed. He himself took his place in the Association, however, and there brought forward a Declaration of Rights which sounds much like the American Declaration of Independence. In this he declared that authority to rule was the gift of the nation, that the sole end of all government was the public good, that all should be taxed in proportion to their means, and at the same rate.

The weeks passed. News came that the king had called out troops to defend himself, then that Necker, the people's favorite, had been dismissed. The attack upon the Bastille followed. After this the National Guard was formed, and its command was placed in the hands of Lafayette. The people looked upon him as so truly their friend that they knew no one else so worthy to receive the key of the Bastille. This he afterwards sent to Washington, and it is now at Mount Vernon. With the key he sent the message: "Give me leave to present you with the main key of the fortress of despotism. It is a tribute which I owe as a son to my adopted father, as an aide-de-camp to my general, as a missionary of liberty to its patriarch."

Lafayette had not the slightest sympathy with riot and destruction and murder. The king was the lawful sovereign of France, and much as Lafayette would have been pleased to see his country a republic, he stood firmly by King Louis. When the mad rush upon Versailles was made, he at the head of several battalions of troops followed the mob to defend the royal family; and to him they owed their lives.

Meanwhile the National Assembly was at work on a constitution, or body of laws which should govern both king and people. They decreed that rich and poor should be taxed at the same rate; that all men should be alike before the law; that there should be no titles of rank, but that every man should be addressed as "citizen," and every woman as "citizeness." The Roman Catholic Church held an enormous area of land in France, larger, it is estimated, than the whole of England, and this was to be taken away for the use of the new government. Every person was to be allowed to follow the religion of his choice, and, whatever his faith, he could not be kept out of office because of it. The whole country was to be divided into departments, and the governor of each was to be elected by the people of that province. Some of the decrees of this Assembly were good; others were not good; but at any rate a constitution had been made, and the king had promised to accept it.

The fall of the Bastille had taken place July 14, 1789, and it was determined to hold a great celebration of the new constitution on the first anniversary of that day. A wide, open space often used for drills, the Champ de Mars, was chosen for the place of the celebration. The time was short and much was to be done to make this ready. To set out with spade or pickaxe and work on the Champ de Mars became the fashionable amusement. Members of the most aristocratic clubs, beggars, priests, soldiers, dancing-masters, matrons and dainty young maidens from families once ennobled, poets, painters, and monks all hastened to show their delight, whether sincere or only politic, in the change of government.

When July 14 had come, there stood on the Champ de Mars a beautiful circular temple made of posts fifty or sixty feet high, each one wound with either white drapery or evergreens, and surmounted by a vase of white lilies. From post to post festoons of green foliage were drawn. More than 300,000 persons were gathered in the temple, many coming before it was fairly daybreak.

At ten o'clock cannon were fired, bells were rung, and a procession led by a band of music marched into the temple. First came Lafayette at the head of the National Guards. He was followed by the electors of Paris, the deputies of the National Assembly, deputies from the different departments, and a long line of men of prominence. In the center of the building a broad flight of steps covered with handsome tapestry led up to an altar adorned with white lilies, and on this lay a Bible and a copy of the Constitution. Near the altar sat the king on his throne, and not far from him was a pavilion for the royal family. Two hundred priests robed in white linen and wearing the national colors, stood on the altar steps. At their head was Bishop Talleyrand, who was to administer the oath.

Mass was celebrated, then the trumpets sounded and the band played as Lafayette ascended the steps of the altar. He laid his sword upon the Bible and raised his right hand toward the sky. The music ceased, and in the silence of the great multitude he said in behalf of himself and the whole army, "We swear to be forever faithful to the Nation, to the Law, and to the King; to maintain to the utmost of our power the Constitution decreed by the National Assembly and accepted by the King." Again the trumpets sounded, and the people shouted, "*Vive la Nation! Vive la Nation!*"

After all the representative bodies had sworn, the king rose in his place, stretched forth his hand toward the altar, and swore to maintain the Constitution with all the power given to him. Then the people shouted, the bands played, the trumpets sounded, and the cannon thundered. One would have thought that there would be nothing but peace and harmony forever after.

But the king was practically a prisoner; the soldiers were ready to mutiny; the popular Necker had to flee to save his life; and when Lafayette tried to save the king from insult, the Guards refused to obey. Lafayette was so disgusted with their behavior that he resigned his command. This aroused the whole state. The Guards begged him to resume his command, the departments begged, the city of Paris begged. "I am thoroughly convinced," said he, "that my comrades love me; but I am still to learn how far they are attached to those principles on which liberty is founded." Finally the mayor of Paris and a deputation from the common council represented to him that for him to resign the command would endanger the state. At this, he yielded, and on the following morning he led his troops to King Louis to make their apologies. Thereupon Danton and Marat and their followers accused Lafayette of having been bribed to stand by the king. Placards were put up throughout the city and pamphlets were published, all to the effect that Lafayette — who had put his life and fortune at the service of liberty — was a supporter of tyranny! He was even accused of helping to plan the king's attempted flight.

Lafayette did all that was possible to keep order and strengthen the government; but the Jacobins had now come into power, and slaughter rather than order was what they wanted. Pictures and busts of Lafayette were destroyed, the dies of the medal which Paris had decreed in his honor were broken up by the common executioner, and a reward was offered for his capture. He saw clearly that he could do nothing more at that time for France. The only way to save his life for future service was to flee.

Holland was then a neutral country, and he set out for Holland, but was captured by the Austrians and kept a prisoner at Olmütz for five years. His cell was most loathsome. A stagnant ditch lay under the tiny window in a wall twelve feet thick. A broken chair, an old table, a heap of straw were its furnishings. When it rained, the water poured in until the captive was drenched to the skin.

In such dens as this, each one worse than those preceding, first in Austria, then in Prussia, the fearless lover of liberty was kept for five years; but he was not forgotten. Washington made a personal appeal to the Emperor of Austria. Other friends, one of them a young man from South Carolina, attempted his rescue. One sure way of liberty was offered him. If he would join the King of Prussia in plotting against France, he would be set free at once. "I am still Lafayette," returned the captive indignantly. His property had been confiscated, and the money sent him by the American minister in France brought him many little comforts, and may have saved his life.

Meanwhile the Reign of Terror was at its height. The mother, sister-in-law, and niece of Lafayette's wife were executed for the crime of noble birth. She herself was imprisoned, but, chiefly through the efforts of the American minister, she was set free. The young wife of fourteen had developed into the strong, wise, determined woman of thirty-two. She sent her son, named for Washington, across the ocean to his father's friend for safety; then she made her way to Vienna and in disguise succeeded in gaining an interview with the emperor. He would not free Lafayette; his wife and two daughters might share his imprisonment if they chose; but if they once entered the prison, they would never be permitted to leave it. Nevertheless, they entered, and what a welcome they must have had! For twenty-two months they remained with him. Then came release. Napoleon Bonaparte, in command of the French forces warring against Austria, demanded as one of the terms of a treaty of peace that Lafayette should be set free. He had been threatened by the Jacobins as a royalist; he had been imprisoned as a republican, whose influence in their own kingdoms was feared by the kings of Europe. He was never tried, and no formal charges were ever brought against him.

Lafayette could do nothing by returning to France; therefore he and his family remained in Holstein from 1797 to 1799, and then made their home a few miles from Paris. During the years of Lafayette's imprisonment, king and queen had been executed, the awful orgy of murder known as the "Reign of Terror" had passed, and in the war with the other nations of Europe the young Napoleon Bonaparte had become the most prominent man in the state. Lafayette liked and admired Napoleon, and was grateful to him for release from prison, but he did not believe that the supreme power which he plainly sought was consistent with liberty. "A free government with you at its head," he said to Napoleon, "I should like nothing better."

During the latter years of his life Lafayette saw many changes in the French government. In 1814, Napoleon was forced to abdicate. Now was the time for the "emigrant" nobles who had left France in the time of Louis XVI. They came back in full force, and by their aid a Bourbon, the brother of Louis

XVI, was set upon the throne. He was called Louis XVIII, for the little dauphin, the son of Louis XVI, is counted as Louis XVII, even though he never reigned.

Before long, Napoleon, who had withdrawn to the little island of Elba, off the coast of Italy, made a sudden return to France. After he was again driven from the throne, Louis XVIII returned from exile and reigned for nine years. Then came his brother, who is known as Charles X. But Charles X had no more sense than to think he could restore things as they were before the Revolution. This brought about revolt, and Charles was obliged to abdicate. The Chamber of Deputies then put upon the throne a descendant of a younger brother of Louis XIV. He was reigning at the time of Lafayette's death.

Soon after the close of the American Revolution, Lafayette had come to the United States for a short time. He begged Washington to visit him in France, but unluckily Washington could not speak French, and he declared that it would be "extremely awkward, insipid, and uncouth" to talk through an interpreter.

Forty years later, Lafayette became the guest of the United States. The country offered him the ship which, in 1777, it had been unable to provide, but he preferred to come by public packet. He landed at New York, then traveled — by carriage, of course — to Worcester, Providence, Boston, and Portsmouth; then back to New York, to Albany, Philadelphia, Trenton, Baltimore, Washington, and elsewhere.

His friends tried to arrange an itinerary, but they might as well have saved their pains, for no one could live up to any itinerary when such crowds were eager to do him honor with cheers and music and banners, triumphal arches, fireworks, and cannon. There were receptions and banquets and addresses and military reviews. There were trembling old veterans of the war eager to shake his hand. In Providence the avenue leading to the court-house was lined with what the old account calls "female youth," dressed in white, waving white handkerchiefs and strewing flowers in his way, "a simple but touching arrangement," the account declares. While Lafayette was in Boston, the corner-stone of Bunker Hill Monument was laid. Daniel Webster was the orator of the day. In the course of his speech, when he addressed to Lafayette personally, as the "sole surviving general officer of Washington's immortal army," words of welcome and appreciation, Lafayette rose from his seat among the Revolutionary officers and remained standing until the close of this portion of the speech.

At Mount Vernon, Lafayette was taken to the tomb of Washington, where he knelt in silent homage to the memory of his friend. He was received by Congress, and at a banquet given him by that body, he gave the toast: "Perpetual union among the United States — it has saved us in our time of danger, it will save the world."

Ten years later, in 1834, Lafayette died. Strange experiences he had met in his life of nearly eighty years. He had known five sovereigns of France, counting the little dauphin. He had known the execution of one king and his queen. He had passed through revolutions and counter-revolutions. He had seen his country ruled by a king and by a mob. He had seen her as a consulate and as an empire. Across the Atlantic he had beheld a little group of colonies win their freedom from the most powerful country of Europe, and their population increased from 3,000,000 to 12,000,000; and in each one of these events he had borne an important and a manly part. Surely it was a worthy and a wonderful life.

CHAPTER XXIII

NAPOLEON THE GREAT AND THE FIRST EMPIRE

A FEW years before Louis XVI and Marie Antoinette came to the throne, a boy was born on the little island of Corsica who became, before many years had passed, far more powerful than they, or any other sovereigns of France ever thought of being. His parents, Charles and Letitia Bonaparte, were Italians, but a few weeks before his birth, Corsica became a part of France, and so the child, who was named Napoleon, was born a French subject.

When Napoleon was ten years old, he was sent to a military school at Brienne. He was small and thin. He had not money enough to dress as well as the other boys. He did not speak French well, for all that he knew of the language was what he had learned in a few months' study. He hated France, because she had conquered his beloved island, but of course he had to keep this hatred to himself. He was proud and a little gloomy, and for some time he kept away from the other boys. The story is told, however, that one very cold winter he proposed building, not a mere "snow fort," but a complicated fortification, made according to military engineering. He divided the school into besieged and besiegers, and the struggle between them was so earnest and followed military tactics so strictly that for many days it was the great entertainment of the people of Brienne to watch the contest.

At fifteen, Napoleon was promoted to the military school of Paris. All expenses here were paid from the royal treasury, and the boys had every luxury, the softest of beds, the most dainty food, and a servant for each to polish his weapons, groom his horse, and wait upon him in every way. This boy, however, did not approve, and he wrote to the governor urging that it would be better for young men expecting to undergo the privations of army life not to attempt to prepare themselves by living in such luxurious surroundings.

In 1785, when Napoleon was sixteen, he passed his examinations for graduation, showing himself especially brilliant in mathematics, and now he wore a sword in all the glory of being second lieutenant of artillery. For some years, however, this was all the glory he could claim, for he was stationed at one place and another in France with no opportunity to show what he could do.

At length, however, his opportunity appeared. As the Revolution progressed, the sovereigns of other countries began to be afraid, as has been said, that it would affect their kingdoms and their thrones. When Louis was put to death, England and Holland delayed no longer, but at once declared war against France. Russia and Spain soon followed their example. In 1793, the troops of the Convention determined to attack the town of Toulon, near Marseilles, which was in the hands of the English and

Spanish. The general in command of the artillery was ill, and the command was given to Napoleon. His years of study had their reward. His management of the artillery was a success, and by a plan which he proposed in a council of war, Toulon was taken.

The young soldier received praise in plenty, but when he asked for an appointment, the reply was always, "You are not old enough." His salary could not be collected, and he actually thought of offering his services to the Turks, then at war with Russia and Austria. "How singular it would be," he said to a companion, "if a little Corsican officer should become King of Jerusalem!"

But the way was opening for him. The French armies were not succeeding in driving the Austrians from Italy. Some one suggested that Napoleon was well informed on the subject, and he was asked to meet with the Committee of Public Safety. Here he showed such knowledge of the Maritime Alps and such skill in planning that he was at length put in command of the war to be waged in Italy against Austria. "The troops are in need of everything," he was told, "and we can furnish you with no money for supplies." "Only give me men enough," responded Napoleon, "and I will ask for nothing more." This was a new kind of commander; but he understood what he was about, and to the troops themselves he said: "Soldiers, you are poorly fed and almost naked. The Government owes you much, but can do nothing. I am about to lead you into the most fertile country in the world. There, great cities and prosperous provinces await you. There you will find honor, glory, and riches. Soldiers of the Army of Italy, shall you lack courage for the enterprise?" They did not lack.

Victory followed victory. One of the most famous was the crossing of the bridge of Lodi under a terrific fire. "It is impossible," said one of Napoleon's officers; but Napoleon retorted, "Impossible? There is no such word in French." The bridge was crossed, and the Austrians were driven back, much to their wrath. "The blockhead knows nothing of the rules of war," declared an Austrian general. "Who ever saw such tactics?" Nevertheless, they were the tactics that won the day. "The boy has done so well," said one of his generals in jest, "that he ought to be promoted. Let us make him a corporal." The troops heard of this, and from that day dates their pet name of the "Little Corporal" for their boyish-looking commander.

After his successes in Italy, Napoleon pushed on into Austria, and was approaching Vienna so rapidly that the emperor asked for peace. The treaty of Campo Formio was signed; and one of its conditions was that Lafayette should be set free.

Not long before Napoleon received his appointment as head of the French troops in Italy, and while he was still in Paris in charge of the defense of the Convention, a winning boy of some twelve years came to see him one day. Napoleon, obeying the orders of the Convention, had taken away all arms from the people of Paris. This boy had come to beg that his father's sword might be given back to him. The father had been guillotined. Napoleon ordered the sword to be returned, and on the following day the boy's mother called to thank the general for his kindness to her son. She had had an eventful life. Some years before, the Viscount Beauharnais had visited the island of Martinique, in the West Indies, and had met the charming young girl named Josephine Tascher. He had married her and brought her to the court of Marie Antoinette. Then came the Reign of Terror, and only the death of Robespierre had saved her from her husband's fate. Beside the boy Eugène who had come to Napoleon, she had also a little daughter, Hortense.

Before long, Napoleon and the young mother of the two children were deeply in love, and three weeks before he set out for Italy, they were married. Throughout the campaign he wore her miniature on a ribbon about his neck, and he never had too much on his hands to write her most affectionate letters. One day he found that the glass over the miniature was broken. This was a bad omen, he feared, and he could not rest till a courier had been sent to make sure that she was well.

Meanwhile there was no government in France that any one could expect to be permanent. The country was ruled by five "Directors," but many people would have been glad to see a king on the throne again or to see almost any change giving them a strong and wise government that would promise to last. But whether people wanted a kingdom or a republic, they were all enthusiastic over the victories of Napoleon, and when he returned, there was a great celebration, so great, indeed, that the Directors felt rather uncomfortable. Authority had changed hands more than once. It was quite possible that this brilliant young commander, to whom the French people were so devoted, might even put the Directors themselves out of office. Already shouts were heard in the streets, "The Little Corporal shall be king! Long live the Little Corporal!" This would never do. Napoleon must be kept out of sight, and then perhaps he would be out of mind. They would order him to invade England.

Napoleon set out with three generals to study the coast of France opposite England. For eight days he examined it; he talked with fishermen and sailors, even with smugglers, and made himself familiar with the whole coast. "It cannot be done," he reported. "It is too dangerous. I will not risk the fate of France upon an attack by sea."

Napoleon had something else to propose, however — and for that matter, he always had "something else" in mind, some bold plan which no other person had thought of; and this time it was to attack England, not on her own shores, but through her possessions in the East, Egypt first of all. He planned not only to conquer, but to colonize, and thus to shut England off from Eastern trade and monopolize it for France. Therefore he wished to take with him a number of scientific men to study the plants and minerals and other wealth of the country. The Directors were ready to agree to almost anything, if they could only get out of the way the man whom they feared, and Napoleon set sail, few, even among the officers, knowing where they were to land.

The English knew that Napoleon had set out with his army for somewhere, but where they could only guess. All they could do was to send Lord Nelson to patrol the waters of the Mediterranean Sea in the hope of meeting the French fleet. Nelson cruised along the Egyptian coast, and then sailed to the northward. Two days later, while he was steering for the Hellespont, the French troops landed safely in Egypt, rushed on to Alexandria, and captured the city. In less than a week, Napoleon had made just laws, had regulated the police system, and had put under way many plans for schools, manufactories, etc. He left three thousand men in charge of the city and set off through the desert for Cairo. It was sixty miles to Cairo, sixty miles of burning, sandy desert; but who could complain when the Little Corporal himself marched at the head of the line, slept on the sand, and ate the same kind of rations that were issued to his men?

Frequently the Mamelukes, the haughty Egyptian troops, mounted on Arabian horses fleet as the wind, dashed down upon them; but Napoleon was equal to even the Mamelukes. He trained his men to form hollow squares at a moment's notice and the word, "Scientists and donkeys to the center!" — for donkeys carried the baggage. These squares, keeping in perfect form, marched wherever they were commanded; but when the moment came to fight, they faced in four directions, artillery at the corners, and the outer ranks kneeling so those within could shoot over their heads. It was not easy to attack a square mass of bayonets, and even when the Mamelukes changed their tactics and made a determined stand, Napoleon won the day. This battle took place in sight of the pyramids; and just before it began, Napoleon made one of his most famous speeches to his troops. He stood, pointing with his sword to the mighty tombs of the ancient kings, and said, "Soldiers, from these summits forty centuries are looking down upon you." It is no wonder that they were aroused to do their best.

In three weeks Napoleon had become master of Egypt, but he formed a government in which the people themselves should rule. He taught them the use of tools that were new to them; he established hospitals, set up a printing press, planned two canals to connect the Red Sea with the Mediterranean, and best of all, won the hearts of the Arabians, for never before had they seen a conqueror who did not abuse them. More than this, he actually seemed to care for them. A poor peasant was slain and his flocks carried off by desert robbers. Napoleon ordered an immediate pursuit and vengeance. "Was the poor wretch your cousin?" asked one of the Arabian chiefs rather scornfully. "He was more than that," Napoleon replied; "he was one whose safety Providence has entrusted to my care."

But even Napoleon did not always have things as

he would. His order to remove the fleet from the Bay of Aboukir, at the mouth of the Nile, had not been obeyed. Nelson came down upon it, and only four ships escaped. This was the Battle of the Nile. Napoleon was deeply disappointed, but all he said was, "We must do greater things than we intended," and a few months later he marched on into Syria. If he could have taken Acre, he might have been able to win Persia and India; but the English and Turks held on to Acre, and a regretful commander led his army back into Egypt.

It had now been many months since Napoleon had heard from France. Sir Sidney Smith, the defender of Acre, either from courtesy or to show that opposition was useless, sent him a great bundle of newspapers. He learned now the story of the year. He learned that almost all the countries of Europe had united against France; that the French had been driven out of Italy; and that all the efforts of France could hardly keep her enemies from her own soil. What should they do? What strong hand could take control? People were asking, "But where is Napoleon? He is strong and wise; he could save us." He might have been slain in the East — no one knew — but France was longing for him, and he was soon on his way to her. With only a little handful of men for a guard, he left the army in Egypt and sailed for France.

When the vessel came near the shores of France and signaled that Napoleon was on board, the whole populace was wild with delight. The people had been fearing an Austrian invasion, but Napoleon would save them. They swarmed over his ship. "The vessel has just come from Alexandria; it may bring the plague," they were warned; but they only shouted jubilantly, "Better the plague than the Austrians!" When Napoleon reached Paris, bells rang, cannon roared, and the streets echoed with his name. In the theaters there was a pause in each play for the announcement, "Napoleon is here!" What he would do, no one could say; but somehow, he would defend them and give them a strong, just government.

The government of France consisted of the five Directors; a senate, which was called the "House of Ancients"; and a house of representatives, or "Council of Five Hundred." In a little more than three weeks, Napoleon had prepared his way. The people and the army were with him, some of the Directors resigned, others favored him. Of the House of Ancients, he demanded the right to draw up a new constitution, and they made no objection. The Council of Five Hundred was then in session. Suddenly they heard proclaimed from the door, "In the name of General Bonaparte, this Assembly is dissolved." There stood Napoleon, and his grenadiers with bayonets lowered, ready to charge. This was Napoleon's *coup d'état*, or blow at the state; that is, a sudden change in the form of government.

By the new constitution France was still a republic, but all power was really in the hands of three consuls, of whom Napoleon was chief. But neither England nor Austria would accept Napoleon as properly the ruler of France. They still declared that a younger brother of Louis XVI was the rightful sovereign. Evidently this must be fought out. Austria was beaten, both in Italy and on her own soil, and she had to sign a treaty agreeing that the Rhine should be the eastern boundary of France. The English were successful in Egypt, but they, too, were ready to sign a treaty the following year.

Now that there was a little freedom from war, Napoleon set to work to care for home duties. The most famous of his works is his Code Napoleon, a revision of the laws of France. It harmonized those that did not agree, and struck out the unfair, oppressive laws. Best of all, it made it clear that in law a man was a man, and that all men were to be treated alike.

Napoleon was now made consul for life. A year or two later, in 1804, the people were asked to vote whether he should be made emperor or not; and in all France there were not three thousand persons who opposed. France was no longer a republic; it had become an empire, and the little boy from Corsica sat upon its throne. To make his position doubly sure, he now asked the Pope, who was quite in his power, to come to Paris and crown him. There were magnificent ceremonies at the Church of Notre Dame, and the Pope anointed the new emperor with the holy oil; but when it came to placing the crown upon his head, Napoleon did that for himself, and then crowned Josephine as empress.

But what did the rest of Europe say to this? How

were they pleased to see on the throne of France this man in no way related to royalty? Of course, they united against him — England, Russia, Austria, and Sweden — all determined to bring back the Bourbon family and put the boundaries of France where they had been in the good old times of the monarchy. Napoleon was longing to invade England, but he had too much to do on the Continent. He made a quick march into Austria, and at the end of 1805, he won a great victory at Austerlitz over the Austrians and the Russians. This brought about many changes in the map of Europe, and sixteen of the German States formed the "Confederacy of the Rhine," with Napoleon for protector. As for England, Napoleon had again decided that he could not cross the "wet ditch," as he called the English Channel, for England was protected by her ships; and already Lord Nelson, off Cape Trafalgar, had destroyed most of the French navy.

War followed war. Napoleon overpowered Prussia and Russia. England stood firm, but there were other ways to attack her than with cannon balls. She had forbidden direct trade between France, Spain, Holland, and their respective colonies. Napoleon now forbade the Continental powers to admit English vessels to their ports or to send ships to England; and this caused an immense loss to English commerce. Portugal did not obey. Thereupon Napoleon seized Lisbon, and then Spain. The King of Spain fled, and Napoleon put one of his brothers on the Spanish throne. Indeed, this conqueror of Europe played with kingdoms and thrones as if they were checkers in a game. One brother he made King of Holland. A brother-in-law was put upon the throne of Naples. Dukedoms and principalities were arranged just as he chose, and were put under the rule of his favorite generals.

But in all of Napoleon's triumphs there was one deep disappointment. The French people had given him the right to name his successor, and he had no child. Between his ambition and his love for Josephine he long hesitated. Then he divorced her, and soon afterwards married Maria Louisa, daughter of the Emperor of Austria — for the emperor did not venture to refuse this powerful suitor. The following year a son was born to them, and to him Napoleon promptly gave the title of "King of Rome."

Except for Spain, Napoleon ruled the Continent from Austria to the Atlantic, and he had an heir to inherit his glory. What more could he ask? But some of those who were watching his career saw here and there little cracks in the mighty structure that he had reared which made them doubt whether his power would last. The kingdoms and dukedoms and principalities which he had formed were not going on as smoothly as he could wish. Of course the princes who had lost their thrones were indignant, and many of their former subjects were restless and discontented. Even in France, Napoleon's power showed signs of weakening. The French gloried in his conquests, but the country was drained of men to fill up the lines of his armies, and the pockets of

NAPOLEON AT THE BATTLE OF FRIEDLAND

even the thrifty French people were drained to pay the cost of these wars. Then, too, Josephine was so gentle and tactful that all the people loved her and they were indignant at the divorce. They had looked upon Napoleon as one of themselves, sorry for their troubles, and bound to do his best to help them; but now that he had allied himself with the imperial family of Austria, they felt that he had deserted their cause and was striving for nothing but his own greatness.

France was tired of war, but Napoleon still saw fields to conquer. The Spanish had not yielded, and the English under the Duke of Wellington had come to help them. It is easy now to look back and see that Napoleon ought to have made sure that Spain was subdued, but Russia, as well as Portugal, had not obeyed his trade laws, and he was bent upon punishing the disobedient country. Straight into Russia he and his army of half a million men marched. He was eager for a great battle, but the Russians had other plans. They slowly withdrew to the northward, burning all foodstuffs as they went. Napoleon followed until he was at Borodino. Then he had his wish. Moscow was only seventy miles away, and the Russians decided to try to overpower the French at Borodino. There was a battle great enough to satisfy Napoleon, and the Russians had to retreat.

Napoleon pursued, for in Moscow there would be food and treasures; but when he came to Moscow, all was dead silence. The food was gone, and the people were gone. In the course of an hour or two, fires broke out in different parts of the city. The wily Russians had kindled them and had carried away or broken up the fire engines. The climate fought for Russia. Napoleon had to retreat as best he could. The cold was intense, and as he and his men ploughed through the deep snowdrifts, half fed and only half clothed, they were attacked by the Russians. Bullets, cold, and hunger did their terrible work, and out of every five men who had gone into Russia, only two ever saw their homes again.

For the sixth time the countries of Europe were united against Napoleon. Wellington had driven the French out of Spain. The allies defeated them at Leipsic, and soon forced their way into Paris. The great Emperor Napoleon was forced to abdicate. The allies were willing to let him keep the title of emperor; but a small empire he reigned over, for he was sent to the tiny island of Elba, eighteen miles long, just off the coast of Italy.

Now was the chance for the friends of the exiled Bourbons. They seized the opportunity to put a younger brother of Louis XVI on the throne, and he took the title of Louis XVIII. But the nobles were as proud and selfish and insolent as they had been in the days of Louis XVI, and the people began to wish that Napoleon was in power again. He was closely watching what was going on in France. He escaped from Elba and landed on the French shores. The troops that had sworn to be faithful to the Bourbon king deserted in a moment and joined the train of Napoleon, and the people were jubilant. Louis XVIII fled, and again Napoleon was Emperor of France.

But again the European countries poured their armies into the empire. Napoleon hurried into Belgium to strike the English and Prussians separately before they could unite. He met the Prussians under Blücher and was victorious, though Blücher's army was not destroyed. At Waterloo, he met Wellington and the English. All day long the fight went on. Grouchy was coming to aid Napoleon; Blücher to aid Wellington. Blücher arrived first. Napoleon made one last charge, but it was useless, and he had to flee to Paris and then to abdicate for the second time. He wished to go to America, but the allies would not permit this. Then he asked to be allowed to live quietly in England; but they knew that, as long as he was in Europe, there would be plots to restore him to the throne of France. He was carried on a British vessel to the little island of Saint Helena, about half as large as Elba. Even here, far away in the South Atlantic, he was carefully guarded and watched lest some plot should be formed to rescue him. Six years later he died with a whispered "Josephine" on his lips. She had died just before he was sent to Elba, and he was glad that she had not seen his final downfall. Maria Louisa had returned to her father's court at Vienna. Napoleon believed that some day his son would rule France, and just before his death he dictated a long letter of advice and affection to be given to him. But the Austrian grandfather did not wish the child to have any connection with France, and he was brought up strictly as an Austrian and was not allowed even to have a French attendant. The baby "King of Rome" was only three years old when he was separated from his father. He worshiped his father's memory, but his questions about him were not answered, and he was never permitted to read his father's letter. At twenty-one he died.

Napoleon had asked to be buried either in France or in Corsica; but it was not until nineteen years after his death that his conquerors would permit his body to be taken from the island of his banishment. It now lies under the dome of the Invalides, in Paris.

CHAPTER XXIV

"NAPOLEON THE LITTLE"

AFTER Napoleon was forced to abdicate in 1814, one Bourbon after another sat on the throne until France was thoroughly tired of both them and the monarchy. First came Louis XVIII, who has been mentioned before. A new charter was made, and Louis was perfectly willing to rule according to its provisions. Indeed, he was more willing than the nobles who had now returned to France. Most of them had had rather a hard time in their exile, and they thought they ought to have privileges enough now to make up for it. They were still afraid of Napoleon, even though he was so closely guarded at Saint Helena, and before long a law was passed that none of the Bonaparte family should ever be allowed to enter France. Much good it did, as will be seen later.

When Louis XVIII died, in 1824, Charles X, another brother of Louis XVI, became king. He had no liking for the charter, and meant to rule just as far as possible in "the good old way." This was the way because of which Louis XVI had lost his head; but Charles did not worry about that. When he saw that his subjects criticized him, then, in the old-fashioned style, he quietly forbade any articles contrary to his views to appear in print. He even punished poets for writing poems in praise of Napoleon, who had now been dead for some years. He ought to have taken a hint from the fact that the National Guards had ceased to cry, "Long live the King!" and now cried, "Long live the freedom of the press!" but no Bourbon ever could take a hint. He disbanded the National Guard, and thought that he had thus quieted all opposition. Then the Chamber of Peers and the Chamber of Deputies made it plain that they did not approve of his acts, and he dissolved them both.

The badge of the empire had been the red, white, and blue cockade; and before long the empire flag was planted over great barricades in the Paris streets, and fighting began. The king understood at last that this rebellion over which the flag of the empire waved, showed that France had had all it would endure of Charles X, and he wisely took his family and boarded a ship bound for England.

There was now a vacant throne, not a very comfortable one, to be sure, but yet a throne, ready for an occupant. Who should it be? Several men whose veins contained more or less of the blood royal were discussed as candidates. The most promising one was a certain Duke of Chartres, afterwards Duke of Orleans, a descendant of the brother of Louis XIV. Lafayette was sent to talk the matter over with him and find out how he was likely to behave if he should be made king.

This Duke of Orleans, Louis Philippe, had made a good record for himself. He had served with honor in the French army until, because of his drop of

Bourbon blood, he had been forced to leave France to save his life. He took refuge in the mountains of Switzerland. His money gave out, and he became a teacher in a school. He gave an assumed name, and the boys who listened to his lectures on geography, mathematics, and history had no idea that "Monsieur Chabaud-Latour" would ever be a candidate for the throne of France. When he left the school, he carried away with him enthusiastic testimonials for the good work that he had done.

He wished to go to the United States, but he was too poor. He wandered about Norway and Sweden, and even made journeys on foot with the Laplanders. At length the way opened for him to go to America, and he landed at Philadelphia. He visited George Washington, went through much of New England, then for several years lived in old England. When Louis XVIII was put upon the throne, he returned to France. He had seen much and thought much. Moreover, he alone of all the Bourbons had learned by what he had seen. He was delighted to find that the French had not forgotten his early services. His large estates, which had been confiscated, were given back to him, and he now devoted himself to a quiet life with his family and the literary men who enjoyed his charming conversation and his hospitable home.

Such was the man whose ideas of what a government should be Lafayette went to find out. Both agreed that the Constitution of the United States was what they would like to see adopted in France, but that the country was not yet ready to become a republic. "It must be in form a monarchy — a popular monarchy," said Lafayette, "but the institutions must be altogether republican." The duke agreed. A few days later he was formally invited to become King of the French. Both chambers of government met together, the cannon were fired and the "Marseillaise" sung. The crown was offered him, and he accepted it and took a solemn oath to obey the charter. He was now a full-fledged King of France, and he moved into the Tuileries.

The throne of France was a rather slippery seat, and to keep on it the new king had to struggle against three parties. One party was satisfied to have the land ruled by a king, but they wanted to choose the king, and they preferred to see the grandson of Charles X on the throne. The second party would have nothing but a republic; and the third would have nothing but an empire with the "King of Rome," whom his Austrian grandfather had made Duke of Reichstag, for emperor.

The Duke of Reichstag died, but not the hopes of the Napoleonists. The head of the Bonaparte family was now Louis Napoleon, son of Hortense and Napoleon's brother. He tried to bring about an uprising in his behalf, but it failed, and the Government sent him off to America. Again he tried, and this time the Government sent him to a fortress at Ham, and sentenced him to remain there for life.

It began to look as if Louis Philippe, and after him his son, would rule France, but a runaway horse changed this prospect, for the son was killed, and *his* little son was only four years old. The chances were that at the death of Louis Philippe — who was now seventy-four — the country would be left with a child for king. This was a condition of affairs which did not please even Louis's strongest friends.

Another difficulty, and the most important of all, was the system of voting, for the result of this was that representatives were elected, not by the whole nation, but only by the wealthy people. The party that wanted a republic set to work to bring about a reform. They took rather original means to arouse the people to see what was needed, for they held great banquets in various towns of France, and at these banquets made speeches explaining what ought to be done. After a while the Government realized what an influence the banquets were having, and when an especially large one, to which fifteen hundred people were invited, was announced to be held in Paris, it was suddenly forbidden.

Now there was uproar, indeed. Mobs gathered in the streets. People armed themselves, threw up barricades across many of the highways, and demanded of every passer-by whether he favored reform or not. The regular troops in trying to keep order fired upon the rioters. This only made matters worse, and on the following day a savage mob surrounded the Tuileries. Even the National Guard now joined the uprising. King Louis Philippe was seventy-five years old; he had neither desire nor power to rule under such circumstances, and he fled. He was more skillful in his flight than Louis XVI, for he did not depart in a big yellow coach, but ordered a cab, put his wife in, and very sensibly and comfortably drove away from the city and its troubles, and entered England as "Mr. Smith."

Here was a whole country without a government. Paris was running wild, and many feared that the awful scenes of 1793 were to be repeated. What was to be done? It was not a politician, but a poet named Lamartine who came to the rescue. He scolded the people good-naturedly and he laughed at them. Best of all, he made them laugh at themselves. Then the victory was won, and they were ready to listen to whatever he had to suggest. Lamartine proposed that a number of men, whom he named, including himself among them, should rule for the time being until a government could be formed. That suited the people. This provisional government decreed that every man, whether rich or poor, should have the right to vote for members of an Assembly. This was fair and just, and nine hundred members were elected. They decided that they had had enough of kings, and that what was wanted was a republic and a president. This president was to be elected as the members had been, that is, by the votes of all the people. Who should it be?

Now when people are wildly excited, if one man keeps calm and serene and has a definite plan, the chances are that the others will accept it. In this case, although there were several prominent candidates for the presidency, there was one man who had long been planning to become ruler of the French, and that man was Louis Bonaparte. He had been sent to Ham for life, as has been said, but in 1846 he had cut off his mustache, made himself four inches taller by wearing high-heeled boots inside wooden shoes, put on a blouse, loose pantaloons, an old blue linen apron, a cap, and a wig of long black hair. He stained his hands red, swung a shelf from his bookcase over his shoulder, and quietly walked out of prison as a carpenter, leaving a dummy in his bed to personate the invalid whom he pretended to be, and so delayed pursuit.

This was the man who appeared in Paris when Louis Philippe abdicated. His special agent set under way a real Napoleonic "propaganda." Pictures, sketches, medals of the first Napoleon and his nephew were scattered throughout France; so were books and pamphlets about the great Corsican. The whole country was made to think of Napoleon, of his greatness and his devotion to France and the interests of the people. It was not then difficult to get the nephew elected to the Assembly, and a little later, to elect him as President of France for four years. Thus was the Revolution of 1848 carried out and for a second time a republic established.

The new president made himself as popular as possible. He wandered about among the workshops of the city with a single attendant, helping with his purse and with kind words wherever he found need, and winning friends everywhere. He put his chief supporters into important offices, and strengthened his power in every possible manner. Before three years had passed, there was heard among the shouts of "Long live the President!" with which he was greeted, an occasional cry of "Long live the *Emperor!*" The minds of the people had been prepared.

One morning when the Parisians awoke, they found the whole city plastered with proclamations. These declared that the Assembly was dissolved and that a new constitution was to be formed. A little later in the day, seventy-eight prominent opponents of the president were arrested, most of them in their beds, and safely stowed away in prison; the National troops took possession of the Hall of the Assembly; and armed forces were stationed at different places in the city. Of course barricades were erected, and bloodshed followed; but within three days the whole affair was over. Louis Napoleon had had a *coup d'état* as well as his uncle. He asked the people to vote whether he should be president for ten years, with what was in reality absolute power. They voted for him — who would not when votes could not be dropped into ballot boxes, but must be given publicly, and when the voter had to march up between two rows of bayonets which were devoted to the service of the new chief? A few months later, the president had himself proclaimed Emperor of France. He was now Napoleon III.

Victor Hugo, the French novelist, declared scornfully that once France was ruled by Napoleon the Great, but now she was ruled by Napoleon the Little. As a whole, however, matters went on fairly well. To be sure, the highest aristocracy of the land were inclined to keep away from the court of the new empire, no matter how brilliant it might be; but, to make up for this, was the fact that the other countries of Europe, delighted to see France in order, recognized, one by one, Louis Napoleon as emperor.

This third Napoleon, however, was as eager as the first Napoleon had been, not only to rule, but to establish a ruling family; and therefore he set about finding himself a wife. Of course he would have been glad to get one from some royal family, but no royal family was anxious to get him. Perhaps this was all the better, he thought, for what was more fitting in the emperor of a democracy than to marry a bride quite without royal blood? The daughter of one of the officers of Napoleon I, Eugénie de Montijo, was beautiful and charming, and soon she became the choice of the emperor. In announcing to the senate that she was to be his wife, Louis shrewdly reminded the senators that the future empress, being partly Spanish, did not possess in France a family to whom it might be necessary to give honors and fortune.

The marriage was celebrated with great brilliancy. Then Napoleon set to work to make France the model state. In Paris he reared splendid buildings, planned a wonderfully excellent system of sewers, made parks and wide, handsome streets and boulevards. He and his empress took many journeys about the empire, noting where a new bridge or a better road or a bit of drainage would be of special advantage. Three years after the marriage, the

Prince Imperial was born; and now there seemed nothing more for the ambitious ruler to ask.

In the bottom of his heart, however, this peace-loving emperor was eager for warfare. War would give people something to talk about. A victory or two would arouse the enthusiasm of his people for their ruler. It might even win over some of those who were opposed to him. At the very least, the opportunity to gain distinction and promotion would bind the army more strongly to its commander. Then, too, if France could become the ally of some other country of the first rank, his own standing at home and in other lands would be much strengthened.

Just at that time, Russia and Turkey had a quarrel. England was opposed to the Czar of Russia, and so supported Turkey, and Napoleon gladly joined England. At the close of the war, he succeeded in having the peace conference held at Paris. He was, of course, the most prominent figure, and both French army and French people as a whole gloried in their leader. Everything was going Napoleon's way. He and the empress visited the English court, and Queen Victoria and Prince Albert visited him. The sovereigns were really becoming quite friendly with the prisoner of Ham.

The next chance for the French army was in Italy. When the European powers rearranged boundaries after Napoleon I was overcome, they gave much of Italy to Austria. One of the Italian princes, Victor Emanuel, and his minister Cavour urged the Emperor of the French to help them against Austria. Napoleon agreed. France and Italy were successful everywhere. One of the battles was that of Magenta; and in America a new color to which the name of "magenta" was given became promptly a favorite.

A few years later, Italy and Prussia made war upon Austria. Prussia won, and now Prussia was much the strongest of the German states.

For twelve years, from 1848 to 1860, Napoleon had had his will. He had reached the height of his glory; the rest of his reign was a slow downfall. The climax of his troubles came in 1870. Prussia was becoming stronger every year. Bismarck, prime minister, the man of "blood and iron," was determined that the many German states should unite, and that Prussia should be at their head. France could not endure the thought of so strong a union of hostile countries being formed at her very doors. Worse yet, the throne of Spain was vacant, and a Hohenzollern prince had expressed himself as willing to accept it if he should be chosen. This would unite Prussia and Spain — possibly against France, and would never do.

France made her objections clear to the Prussian Government, and the prince agreed not to become a candidate for the throne. The French ambassador then urged King William to make a formal agreement to the effect that no Hohenzollern prince should ever occupy the throne of Spain. This the king refused to do. He telegraphed an account of the interview to Bismarck, allowing him to make the telegram public or not, as he thought best. Bismarck rewrote it, leaving the facts, but changing the tone, and, as he himself said, "The original was an order to retreat, now it is a summons to charge." He had so "edited" the telegram that France felt insulted and declared war. This was just what Bismarck had been working to bring about. He had seen to it that the Germans were well prepared for war, and he knew that the French were not.

The emperor was seriously ill and often suffered intensely. He felt no enthusiasm for battle, but he and the crown prince of fourteen years at once joined the army. Only six weeks later came the battle of Sedan, and he had to telegraph to Eugénie, "The army is vanquished and in captivity. I am myself a prisoner." The tutor of the young prince succeeded in getting the boy safely to England.

Then the German army marched straight through France and besieged Paris. For four months her brave people bore cold and hunger; but only actual starvation could make them yield. In January, 1871, they surrendered. The Germans were already in possession of beautiful Versailles. In the superb Hall of Mirrors, King William I of Prussia was proclaimed German Emperor. Bismarck had his wish; the German states had united, Prussia was the chief among them, and the King of Prussia and his children after him would rule the German empire. The victors allowed a three-weeks' armistice so that a government might be formed, and there might be some authority with which they could treat. France was now obliged to agree to pay $1,000,000,000 as indemnity, and to surrender Alsace and the greater part of Lorraine, which she had captured in the days of Louis XIV.

For everything that had gone wrong the French blamed the Empress Eugénie even more than the emperor, and she had had to flee from the Tuileries to escape from a furious mob. "She was always extravagant," they declared. "She is not a born Frenchwoman, and she cares nothing for France." By the help of her American dentist, she escaped from Paris and made her way to England. Queen Victoria showed her all sympathy and kindness. Her husband was kept a prisoner for a few months, then he joined her, but lived only two years after the end of the war. The Prince Imperial, whose birth had been such a delight to the Napoleonists of France, was trained in an English military school and graduated with honors. When the Zulu War broke out in South Africa, he joined the English army and was slain. The Empress Eugénie still lives in England (1920), a sad, fragile woman of ninety-four, but with what a life to remember!

CHAPTER XXV

IN THE DAYS OF MARSHAL FOCH

It was one of the terms of peace at the close of the Franco-German War that the German army should march into Paris in triumph. They marched in, to be sure, but there was not much triumph about the march, for there was no one to see it. The Parisians not only kept off the streets, but they pulled down the curtains.

The more the French people thought of their defeat, the more indignant they were. They blamed everybody. They were furiously angry with the Assembly for making such a peace, and with the president of the Assembly for signing it. He was Thiers, the historian, and in stupid revenge the mob burned his valuable historical library. They established a government of their own, which they called the Commune, they shut the city gates against the Assembly, and they burned the beautiful Tuileries and many of the most stately buildings of the city. At length, the troops of the Assembly forced their way into Paris and established order; but only barely in time, for the people were beside themselves with anger and disappointment, and they were about to set up a guillotine and repeat the horrors of the Reign of Terror. To bring such a mob to order was not an easy thing to do, but it was done. Another thing which was not easy was paying the enormous indemnity. Thiers, and, indeed the rest of the world, did not think it would be possible to make up the sum within the three years allowed; but the thrift of the French people paid the final franc in less than half the time, and they saw with great pleasure the last soldier of the German army of occupation march over the border.

The French could pay this enormous sum of money, and they could rebuild some of the structures torn down by the Paris Commune, but they could not recover the lost Alsace and Lorraine. German laws were at once put in force in the two provinces, and it was strictly forbidden to use French in the schools.

France was now a republic. A new constitution was prepared, and in 1875 it was formally accepted by the country. There were no more revolutions, and for thirty-nine years France prospered. Like other countries, she had her troubles, but she had also her glories, and she was making a steady progress in all lines when suddenly the World War, the most terrible conflict of all time, was sprung upon her. The Prussian military party had long been eager for war. Germany was perfectly prepared. Every able-bodied man in the land had been trained as a soldier; guns and ammunition were ready; even large quantities of hospital supplies. Her plans were carefully laid. She would attack France through Belgium, then subdue Russia and England; she would open the way "from Berlin to Bagdad" and the conquest of the East; she would make a wide strip through Europe, from the Baltic Sea to the Mediterranean, her own domain; then she would cross the ocean and extort ransom from the large coast cities of the United States; the rest of the world could be conquered at her leisure.

Germany alone was prepared for war, but Belgium, France, England, and Russia did their best. At the end of 1914, after five months of warfare, the most that could be said was that Germany had not conquered Europe. At the end of 1915, the report was not so very much better. Germany's opponents had taken some of her colonial possessions, but on the Continent she had not lost a foot of land, and had been successful in several places to the east of Austria. In 1916, the powers allied against Germany had held Verdun in spite of every effort made to conquer it. They had been successful on the Somme, in Armenia, and on the sea. On the other hand, they had failed in the East.

In 1917, the United States entered the war. The piratical U-boat warfare of Germany had destroyed much shipping, but it had brought in this new ally. Germany had made gains in Italy, and Russia had crumbled; but the Allies had captured Bagdad and Jerusalem. And so the news came. The side that gained one day lost the next. The whole struggle had come to a deadlock. Germany must yield in time, but when? How long must the terrible slaughter continue?

Now in every war in which different nations are allied, there is one lesson which has to be learned afresh, and it is that there must be one supreme commander. Thus far the Germans had had a great advantage in that they were under one control. The Allies coöperated, but the army of each nation had its own commander, and unless two commanders were near enough to consult, every one went in great degree his own way. It was now agreed that one man must be in supreme command, and the man chosen was Ferdinand Foch.

He was born in 1851, in a little village in the Pyrenees, not so very many miles from where the knight Roland laid down his life in Charlemagne's day. The boy's grandfather had been one of the guards of Napoleon I, and his favorite great-aunt was the widow of a general who had been viceroy of Holland in the days of the First Empire. Stories upon stories of warfare the small boy heard, and he delighted in them all, even when his forgetful great-aunt insisted upon his remembering events that had happened long before he was born.

The little Ferdinand and his brothers and sisters were taught to obey without a question, and there is a rather pathetic story of his struggling to be obedient and eat peas, which he disliked, and saying tearfully, "My heart comes right up in my mouth when I crack them; but I really want to obey, and so I swallow them at one gulp."

At eighteen, he went to a college at Metz, and two years later he had something harder to endure than eating peas, for the Germans had triumphed over France in the Franco-German War. The victors took possession of the city and even of part of the college; and the young student, who had just spent six months in the French army, was obliged to live in the same building with them, and submit to their demands and insults with outward deference and inward wrath.

Long afterwards he said that in those days he vowed that Alsace and Lorraine should be once more in the hands of France, and that the French should not remain a conquered people. His aim was to prepare to help in the rescue of his country, whenever the time should come, and he did fine and earnest work at the Polytechnic School in Paris. After graduating, he held one military position of honor after another for several years, and then was made professor at the War School in Paris.

This new professor had not forgotten his boyish vows. The young officers who listened to his lectures were to become, not merely part of an army, but the brains of the French army, authorities in whose hands would rest making plans for the forces that might some day be called on to defend France. It is no wonder that he taught with an eagerness to give them his best. He taught them that, although the commander-in-chief *is* the commander-in-chief and all others must obey him, yet difficulties will arise in carrying out the commander's orders, and therefore, to obey efficiently, an officer must be able to think for himself. He taught them that they must study the enemy, learn to guess what he is about to do, and watch for his weak points. He taught them that victory is first of all a matter of belief; that the army which firmly expects to win the fight is well on the way to success. He taught them to be cheerful. "Depression is a confession of intellectual weakness," he said. "Depression has lost more battles than any other cause."

The great menace to France was Germany, and Foch analyzed with his students the war of 1870, noting carefully the mistakes on both sides, and making plan after plan to oppose any German invasion. He had not expected Germany to toss her agreements aside and march through Belgium, but he had a plan carefully thought out to oppose her even there. The Germans said sneeringly that Foch learned all his strategy from them. Even if this had been true, it is not what a man learns, but how he uses it that counts.

Such was the man who, in March, 1918, became commander-in-chief of the Allied armies. He had already made a fine record at the Marne and at Ypres. Every one knew the story of his famous dispatch to Marshal Joffre at the Marne: "My right wing has been driven back; my left wing is crushed; I shall attack with my center." Another tale is that, when one of his officers hesitated to advance because his men were worn out, Foch responded, "So are the Germans. Attack!"

For the spring of 1918 the Germans had prepared to make a gigantic offensive on the Western Front. They made it, but unluckily for them the methods of this new commander-in-chief were different from theirs. They believed in elaborate preparation, then a drive, then more preparation, then another drive, and so on. Foch believed in "keeping on going on," in hammering away at them steadily, first in one place, then in another, wherever they showed signs of weakness.

The Americans came just in time to turn the tide that threatened to overwhelm Paris; and at Sedan, where, half a century earlier, Napoleon III had been obliged to give up his sword to William of Prussia, the final blow was struck. The French were at work west of the American troops; the English were striking hard in Flanders; in Siberia, Palestine, on the Italian Front, and in the Balkans the Germans were losing. Turkey and Austria were out of the war. Germany begged for an armistice, which was in reality an unconditional surrender. The terms of this surrender, severe, but just and strictly in accordance with military rule, were read to the German representatives by Marshal Foch. He had kept the vow of his school-days. Alsace and Lorraine were rescued; France was no longer a conquered nation. Foch rarely talks of his victories, but when he does, he always ends reverently with, "We were the instruments. God was there."

THE END

The Riverside Press
CAMBRIDGE . MASSACHUSETTS
U . S . A